COMPETITIVE DRILLS
FOR WINNING BASKETBALL

COMPETITIVE DRILLS FOR WINNING BASKETBALL

Jan Lahodny

PARKER PUBLISHING COMPANY
West Nyack, New York 10994

Library of Congress Cataloging-in-Publication Data

Lahodny, Jan.
   Competitive drills for winning basketball.
   ISBN 0-154949-9
    1. Basketball—Coaching.   I. Title.
  GV885.3.L32   1986   86-513
  796.32'3'077   CIP

Printed in the United States of America

10   9

ISBN 0-13-154949-9

ATTENTION: CORPORATIONS AND SCHOOLS

Parker Publishing Company books are available at quantity discounts with bulk purchase for educational, business, or sales promotional use. For information, please write to: Prentice Hall Career & Personal Development Special Sales, 113 Sylvan Avenue, Englewood Cliffs, NJ 07632. Please supply: title of book, ISBN number, quantity, how the book will be used, date needed.

PARKER PUBLISHING COMPANY
West Nyack, NY 10994

A Simon & Schuster Company

On the World Wide Web at http://www.phdirect.com

Prentice-Hall International (UK) Limited, *London*
Prentice-Hall of Australia Pty. Limited, *Sydney*
Prentice-Hall Canada Inc., *Toronto*
Prentice-Hall Hispanoamericana, S.A., *Mexico*
Prentice-Hall of India Private Limited, *New Delhi*
Prentice-Hall of Japan, Inc., *Tokyo*
Simon & Schuster Asia Pte. Ltd., *Singapore*
Editora Prentice-Hall do Brasil, Ltda., *Rio de Janeiro*

Dedication

To my husband, Glenn . . . for his love, understanding, and total support of my career.

To my nine-month-old son, "Buck". . . for much happiness and help as co-author of this book.

To my parents, my sister and her children . . . for always letting me know that they thought I was the greatest.

To my best friend, Gina . . . for reminding me that there is more to life than basketball.

To my coaching associates . . . for unselfishly sharing their knowledge of the game.

To my former and present coaching staffs . . . for tolerating my eccentricities, my ego and other imperfections.

To my spirit and spiritual leader, Mona . . . for teaching me about God's love and power.

To my players, past, present and future . . . for making my dreams a reality.

About the Author

Jan Lahodny is the girls' basketball coach at Victoria High School in Victoria, Texas. She attended Temple Junior College on a basketball scholarship for two years and then continued her basketball career at the University of Texas in Austin where she received her Bachelor of Science Degree in Physical Education.

Following graduation, Coach Lahodny took over the duties of head coach at Shiner High School. During her six-year tenure, her teams captured three district championships. In 1972, her team advanced to the regional finals, and in 1974, her team received state runner-up honors.

During her first year at Victoria, Coach Lahodny directed her team to a state runner-up title with a season record of 33 wins and 2 losses. In 1978, her team once again received state runner-up honors with a season record of 36 wins and 2 losses. In 1979, Lahodny directed her team to the Class AAAA State Championship. The 1981 season saw her capture the District Championship with a 31 win and 5 loss ledger. In 1982, her team won the Class AAAAA State Championship title posting a 35 win and 2 loss record, and in 1983, her team logged a 36 win and 2 loss record capturing State Runner-up Honors. Her team once again captured State Runner-up Honors in 1985 with a 30-7 record.

Coach Lahodny has coached the Texas South All-Star Team three times, was selected the 1982 Texas Association of Basketball Coaches Girls' Coach of the Year, and has compiled a career record of 418 wins and 114 losses during her sixteen-year coaching career. She recently received her Master's Degree in Education from the University of Houston in Victoria.

Introduction

This is not a book of new or fancy drills. The drills given are the standard drills used by basketball coaches all over the world. What is unique about the techniques in this book is that they will teach you how to get your players to give maximum effort in every practice session throughout the entire season. Through a system of competitive drilling, you will learn how to make your practice sessions more interesting and more challenging to your players.

While I was in college, one of my teammates made this remark to me, "I hated basketball practice when I was in high school. I could have written the workout. We did the same drills every day. It would get so boring." As a beginning coach, this statement came to haunt me.

If you are like most coaches, you have certain drills that you feel your team must practice every day. This repetition can become extremely monotonous to your players. For many seasons, I would see my players show great enthusiasm the first few weeks of practice and then watch that enthusiasm dwindle down to actual yawning in practice.

What could I do to make practice more interesting, more challenging to my players? How could I keep their enthusiasm alive? At first, I tried a variety of drills—changing them from day to day or week to week. However, this did not prove satisfactory for several reasons. First of all, there was the time element. To explain a new drill and how to execute it correctly takes time. And, as we all know, proper utilization of time is most essential to a good workout. I quickly saw that I was losing too much time every day explaining new drills. Furthermore, in my effort to devise new daily drills, I saw myself slipping away from the drills that I knew would best teach the skills that were necessary for success in our style of play. Finally, I realized that changing the workout routine did not generate the enthusiasm among my players that I had expected.

Enthusiasm and motivation seemed to be elusive intangibles that, I was certain, were the difference between winning teams and losing teams. I began to doubt my ability as a coach. Maybe I didn't have the personality to be a great coach. My pre-game and half-time talks were pretty good, but at day-to-day motivation I was a failure. I tried it all— chants, posters, locker-room slogans, etc. These gimmicks would light a spark, but never set my practice sessions on fire.

Then I realized that I had not clearly identified the problem and that player enthusiasm per se was not exactly what I was looking for in a good workout. What I wanted was a 100 percent effort from every player during every minute of my workout. The idea that enthusiastic players would give that 100 percent effort was a noble idea, but it was not in reality a truth. Hard work was the clear and simple answer to my problem. Therefore, I created a system of totally competitive drilling.

What is competitive drilling? Competitive drilling simply means that every drill used in our practice session is in the form of a game or a challenge. If the game is not won or the challenge not met, the players have to run, jump, or put forth some type of physical effort for not having succeeded. A very elementary example of a game drill is our half-court layup drill. The squad is divided into a blue team and a red team. The blue team is shooting at the basket on the north end of the court while the red team is shooting on the south end of the court. There is a shooting line and a rebound line on each end. The players are instructed to alternate lines during the drill. The two managers who operate the scoreboard put two minutes on the clock. The drill begins on the coach's whistle. One point is awarded per basket and is recorded on the scoreboard. When the buzzer sounds, the losing team goes to the line to run a wind sprint under four seconds, or perhaps, one wind sprint for every point by which they lost. The same drill could be done as a challenge drill by instructing the group that they will have to make 35 baskets during the two-minute period or they will have to run. In this type of drill, it may happen that neither team has to run if they meet the challenge.

The implementation of a system of competitive drilling from this example may seem very simple to you, but there are many intricate details which must be taken into account to gain the desired results. The purpose of this book is to teach you how to develop your own philosophy of competitive drilling and how to implement it into your program successfully. You'll discover how to get maximum performance from your players in every practice session which will help you develop those long-awaited championship teams!

This book is a must for basketball coaches who want their teams to develop a keenly competitive attitude. If you implement the competitive drills described in this book into your program, you will obtain the following positive results:

1. You will get a 100 percent effort from each player in every workout throughout the entire season—which is the "real" secret to consistently developing championship teams.

2. You will utilize your practice time more effectively. The timing of each drill will automatically set up a time schedule for your workouts.

3. You will find your teams scoring more and more frequently right on the buzzer. The timing of all your drills will make your players extremely conscious of the clock, and thus create in them a very real sense of what can actually be done in three seconds, five seconds, etc.

4. Most importantly, you will find your team winning close games more consistently. Since the implementation of competitive practice drills into my program, the seven teams that I've sent to the state championship have won 72 percent of their games that were decided by four points or less.

Table of Contents

1

How to Put the Philosophy of Competition into Practice

To develop a philosophy of coaching, you must first have a goal in mind. Our goal—referring to my coaching staff and me—is to get our players to give 100 percent effort in every drill in every practice session throughout the entire season. The importance of this goal should not be underestimated. If you, as a coach, can accomplish this goal, then you will have instilled in your players the ingredient most essential to winning—the ability to compete.

The ability to compete is not an inherent trait of female athletes in our society. It must be taught on a daily basis. That is why *all* practice sessions should be of a competitive nature. Day-by-day, minute-by-minute competition, however, can unleash many undesirable qualities such as anger, cheating, improper execution, unnecessary roughness, etc., among team members. It is, therefore, necessary to enforce a strict philosophy of team discipline, proper execution of skills, and unity.

A PHILOSOPHY FOR TEAM SUCCESS

Discipline is not a responsibility to be shouldered by the coach alone. Every player in the program needs to be responsible for the discipline of the team. To impress the importance of team discipline upon our players, nearly all of our team rules are so written that if one player misbehaves, the entire team suffers the consequences. For instance, if someone throws a temper tantrum during practice or during a game, the entire group must run a set number of sprints. It may seem unfair for the group to have to run because of the loss of control of one individual, but basketball is a team sport. Should one person receive a technical foul during the course of a game resulting in a loss, the entire team loses the game, not one individual.

We advise our players to encourage their teammates to control their emotions, to come to practice on time, to put forth 100 percent effort into all practice sessions—in other words, always to behave and perform like a champion. Once you have convinced your players that in the long run they will suffer because of a teammate's lack of control, desire, or dedication, you will have succeeded in putting into effect the greatest motivator among young people today—peer pressure. The group will let offending teammates know that they do not appreciate their behavior, and chances are the coach will never have to single out an individual again. The team will begin to discipline itself.

1

How to Encourage Proper Execution of
Fundamental Skills

The proper execution of offensive and defensive techniques are critical to a team's success. These techniques will of course vary according to the coach's philosophy. In our program, we feel that each player must be a master of the following techniques: low post moves, post defense, guarding the dribbler, defending a perimeter player without the ball, defending a perimeter player in the scoring area with the dribble left, blocking out, free throw shooting, and the offensive concepts of pass opposite, wing penetration, post penetration, guard cut and fill, and hi-lo action. A coach can demonstrate and instruct players how to perform certain fundamental skills correctly, but this does not guarantee their proper execution.

The best motivator we have found is a system we call "Earning Your Uniform." Each player in the program earns their uniform—one piece at a time—by properly executing certain fundamental skills. For instance, there are three post moves that have to be mastered before a player will be issued her game shirt. To make this system work, we have our managers videotape every practice session during the pre-season practices. The tapes are then reviewed by the coaches after school. Evaluations of each player's performance are made, and suggestions for improvement are posted on the wall. There is quite a furor among the players as they strive to execute the fundamentals perfectly, so that they are able to earn their complete uniform by the first game of the season.

How to Encourage Unity

Unity among *all* members of our program is encouraged by a standing rule stating that everyone in the program (Freshman, Junior Varsity, and Varsity) has to run if a loss is suffered by any of the teams in the high school program. For instance, if the Freshman team loses a game, during the following practice, all three teams have to run five horses (see Chapter 3). If the Junior Varsity loses, ten horses have to be run; if the Varsity suffers a loss, they must run fifteen horses. This tactic helps promote enthusiasm in the performance and success of their fellow teammates, regardless of the level of competition. For example, Varsity players are very willing to lend a hand to Freshman and Junior Varsity players who are struggling with a weakness in their playing style. In addition, instructions on how to execute fundamental skills properly are available to underclassmen by upperclassmen, as well as by coaches. Thus, a coaching staff of three is enlarged to a staff of thirty-three.

The methods described above may seem rather callous, but there is little doubt among team members that they are necessary and effective. A peer pressure type of discipline, proper execution of fundamental skills, and unity are the building blocks of team success in our program.

To make certain that players—and parents—understand our philosophy for team success, the coaching staff has carefully prepared a set of team rules and has outlined the methods that are used to implement them. On the first day of school, these handouts are given to each player to be taken home for their parents' signatures. The signature forms are returned to the coach and kept on file. Therefore, it is well established in advance how disciplinary situations, earning a uniform, and losing will be handled.

FOUR CRITERIA OF A WINNING WORKOUT

Planning your practice sessions should be a step-by-step process. You should always keep in mind the following criteria of a good workout:

1. Using time efficiently;
2. Using floor space efficiently;
3. Cutting down on explanations and demonstrations; and
4. Involving every player in practice at all times.

Let us examine each of these more closely.

Using Time Efficiently

You must sell your players on the idea that a short, vigorous, meaningful workout is much better than a long, drawn-out session. In order to do this, a coach must be well organized. Also, you should expect your players to start practice immediately. During our in-school practice sessions, the deadline for each player to be on the floor ready to practice is 11:45 A.M. by the gym clock. Furthermore, each player must be at her assigned spot on the floor. For the teaching of basic fundamental skills in early pre-season, we use a mass drill formation for "follow-the-leader" type drills. Later in the year, each player is assigned to a particular basket for shooting-form drills. This "spot" assignment conveniently facilitates roll-check by the managers as the drills begin. Then, as explained before, should anyone be late to practice or loafing during the drills, the entire group has to run.

In addition, players are not allowed to walk from line to line while performing their drills or while moving from one drill to another. Everyone is expected to "hop" to their assignments at a full run.

Since all of our drills are done in competition, it is necessary for certain team members to wear practice vests. These assignments are posted on the wall by the coach prior to practice, so that as the players come into the gym they will know what color practice vest to put on before taking the floor.

If players are to be divided up into certain teams for the practice, a list of the teams should be posted and numbered, so that time does not have to be taken up during the actual workout. The coach simply calls out, "Team one to this basket. Team two to the other end." It is also a good idea to number your baskets, if you are using all six. This cuts down on confusion as to where to go and, over a period of time, it will help to save a substantial amount of time.

We stress the importance of utilizing every minute of our practice time. If, for example, we lose as little as five minutes a day, in six days of practice we lose thirty minutes. In four weeks' time, we lose two hours. In four months, we lose eight hours. Since most of the schools in our conference begin school a week earlier than we do, we have to play "catch up," and cannot afford to waste a minute.

If we have to stop practice to handle a discipline problem, we emphasize to our players that today one of our rival schools got ahead of us. Rather than taking up practice time to talk about a team problem, we often outline the problem in a letter. We then put it in all the players' lockers, so that they may quickly read it while dressing. All other announcements such as the time to leave for an out-of-town game, after-school practice times, etc., are posted on the bulletin board next to the dressing room door.

The most important technique that assures maximum utilization of time, however, is the timing on the scoreboard clock of all practice drills. The advantages of this method of practice are:

1. It keeps the drills short, and therefore interesting to the players.

2. It keeps the coach from spending too much time developing skills in one area at the expense of others.

3. It improves player performance.

Every day, in every drill, players are placed in win or lose situations. Time after time, they must come down the floor to try to score the winning basket with three, four, five, etc., seconds left on the clock. This makes them realize what can be accomplished in a set amount of time, e.g., whether the ball must be put up from 20 feet out, or if there is enough time to drive the ball for a closer shot. With this technique, the players quickly become aware of how best to utilize the time remaining on the clock and how to perform under pressure.

Using Floor Space Efficiently

Once again, the coach must be well organized to utilize all of the floor space that a practice facility affords. All activities should be set up in such a manner that none of the players have to stand in line for more than five seconds at a time watching other players. This may seem difficult when a coach is working with a large group. But you must, with a little creativity, strive to utilize every basket, the bleachers, the stage, or whatever else is available to keep the players moving.

A good example of this would be our one-on-one drill which we use during our in-school practice sessions. During this period, all three teams—Freshmen, Junior Varsity, and Varsity—work out. This includes about 40 to 50 girls. The Freshmen players are divided into a red team and a blue team, and a combination of Junior Varsity and Varsity players are divided into a red team and a blue team. The Freshmen are instructed to play one-on-one from the free throw line on the side baskets, while the Junior Varsity play full court one-on-one on the main floor. The blue teams shoot at the two baskets on the north end of the gym, and the red teams shoot at the baskets on the south end (see Diagram 1-1). (A detailed description of this drill will be given in Chapter 5.)

The managers are instructed to put five minutes on the scoreboard clock and to keep score for each team. One point is awarded for each basket. Red is home and blue is visitor. The players are informed that the losing team will have to run a "dribbling horse" (explained in Chapter 3) under 45 seconds.

Players rotate from offense to defense and vice versa. To assure that no player is standing in line for more than five seconds—and also to make the drill more competitive than by simply determining a winning team—the players have to run during the course of the drill for individual failures. If they are on offense and they do not make the basket, they will have to run a bleacher. If they are on defense and the offensive player scores, they will have to run a bleacher. Thus, one of the two has to run. The players must zigzag the bleachers, as shown in Diagram 1-1, and return to the appropriate line before their next turn. And, of course, if someone misses her turn because she was not hustling, the entire group has to run for it at the end of the drill.

This drill may seem like a "Chinese Fire Drill" with people clamouring up and down the bleachers, not to mention the activity on the floor, but in reality, it is well organized and helps eliminate lapses of concentration by players standing idly in line. Conditioning and motivation to succeed are added benefits to this method of practice.

Cutting Down on Explanations and Demonstrations

All coaches must of course instruct their players as to how they want things done, but every effort should be made to spend a minimal amount of time in all explanations and demonstrations. Remember, players will learn more quickly by doing than by listening and watching.

There are several techniques that can help to expedite coaching instructions:

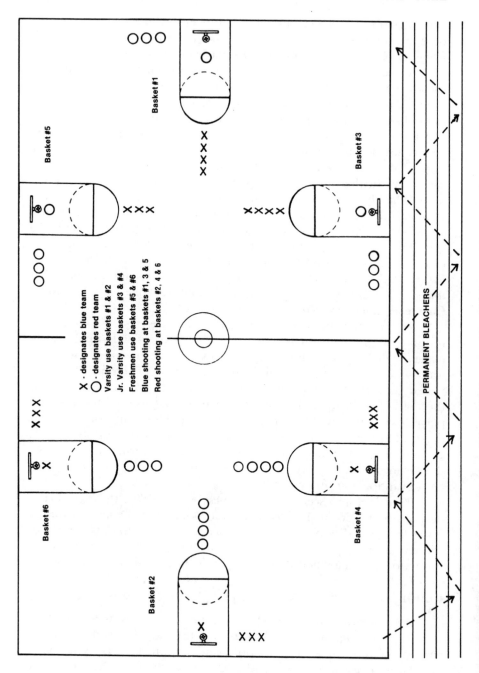

X - designates blue team
O - designates red team
Varsity use baskets #1 & #2
Jr. Varsity use baskets #3 & #4
Freshmen use baskets #5 & #6
Blue shooting at baskets #1, 3 & 5
Red shooting at baskets #2, 4 & 6

Diagram 1-1

1. Explain clearly but briefly, and only *one time*, how to execute a certain fundamental skill. Then put the players immediately into action on the *one* drill the coaching staff has decided is the *best* drill for teaching this particular fundamental skill. Explanation time is greatly reduced by using only one drill to teach a particular skill.

2. Prepare a checklist for proper execution of a particular skill. An example of the checklists used in our program is as follows:

EXECUTING TWO-ON-ONE SITUATIONS PROPERLY

Rule #1—If an open player is dribbling toward you, clear to the other side of the basket and wait for a pass or position yourself for a rebound.

Rule #2—A two-on-one situation lasts only for an instant. You have time for only one pass. A bounce pass is usually the most effective as the defender is primarily interested in stopping the shot.

Checklist: Offensive Player

1. The open player must make the sole defender pick her up. She must be willing to drive in for the layup if the defender does not stop her.

2. The guarded player clears to the other side of the basket when the dribbler starts the drive toward her.

3. If the defender stops the drive, the girl with the ball hits the other girl with a short, crisp bounce pass. She then positions herself for a rebound.

4. If the defender does not stop the drive, the girl on the opposite side positions herself for the rebound.

Checklist: Defensive Player

1. The defensive player must stop the drive first.

2. The defender uses defensive fakes to try to get the dribbler to pick up the ball as far away from the basket as possible.

3. If help has not arrived, she quickly falls back on the girl under the basket to stop the short pass and forces her to shoot the longer range, lower percentage jump shot.

4. She must fight the offensive players for rebound position.

Frequently, at the end of a practice session, we give a brief oral test covering the items on the checklist and have the entire team run for each incorrect answer. For instance: "Brown, in a two-on-one situation, you have time for how many passes?" "One." "What kind of pass should it be, Jones?" "A bounce pass." "Reynolds, what is the first responsibility of the defensive player in a two-on-one situation?" "Stop the bounce pass to the player she is guarding." "Wrong, she must stop the drive first!" "Okay, everyone line up for one minute of forward and backward sprints!"

3. Issue certain equipment only after the criteria in the checklist have been met by the individual player. For instance, our players do not receive their warm-up pants until they have shown acceptable execution of a two-on-one situation in our daily drill. Evaluations of videotaped practice sessions are posted daily on a chart (see Diagram 1-2) so that players can readily see what areas of their game need improvement. If a player earns a particular piece of equipment, it is so indicated on a master chart (see Diagram 1-3) which is displayed on a wall next to the coaches' office.

4. Make the individual players immediately "pay the price" for failure to perform successfully. As explained before, in our one-on-one drills, the players have to run a bleacher if they don't score or if someone scores on them. A player who is constantly having to run often becomes concerned about what it is she is doing wrong. She will frequently come to me during the drills and say, "Coach, watch me this time. I don't know what I'm doing wrong." A very unique teaching situation has been created—you have the player's undivided attention and she wants to learn. Therefore, I quickly offer suggestions as to what she needs to work on to improve her performance and she immediately returns to the drill.

5. Never stop the entire drill or practice session to give instruction to one player, unless it is something that would benefit the entire group. During summer camps, I get extremely aggravated when working with other coaches who will stop the entire practice session while he or she spends three to four minutes—and sometimes longer—correcting one individual. Any correction or explanation should be made as quickly as possible or players should be taken aside for individual instruction.

6. Demonstrations by the coach should be kept to a minimum. Coaches who were once-talented players themselves often get so carried away in giving demonstrations that they take away much valuable participation time from the players.

Involving Every Player in Practice at All Times

Although many of the previous discussions concerning maximum utilization of time, maximum utilization of floor space, and minimal amount of explanation time also serve as suggestions for giving players the maximum amount of participation time, other helpful practice methods include the following:

TURNER	WALLACE	WARE	ONE-ON-ONE FULL COURT SEPT 10TH		
KB EL	RU KB BT	KB *Stop* BT *jumping on the shot*			
LEE KB BT H	**ORTIZ** KB-R-RU *Terrible* BT EL-D-L	**ORSAK** RU *Need* L *to get your head in the drill!*	**RAB** SS KB EL BT L	**ROSENQUEST** *Good, but you won't get have until you stop reaching!*	**STRYK** *Good, but running too much.*
AVILA RU BU R	**CAVAZOS** SS L D EL	**CORLEY** SS 45 R RU *Terrible*	**GARLEY** R *Reaching* R *way too* R *much!* BO	**GILSON** FT 45 SS BT	**KLAGES** H BO KB BT
NUGENT SS D L BU H BO	**OWENS** RU *Need to shuffle, not run + stop* R	**SPEARS** D KB L BT H	**SWOBODA** BO BT BU KB L	**TERRY** SS H L EL	**TTOELL** *Good, but still R too much*
BANKSTON *Don't give up* ✓ −	**BATTALORA** SS L	**DAVIS** KB BT FT H	**GREEN** BO SS KB	**KARM** SS 45 RV H	**MOELLER** RU SS R
ROSS ✓ +	**WIMBISH** *Feet need to stay on ground* ✓ −	**RUSSELL** ✓ +	**EICHMAN** BT H D	**GOODE** EL BU	**HILLER** R D SS
SNEED R H	**VRAZEL** RU L 45	**ALKEK** BT 45 RU	**CONAWAY** BT KB FT	**BUCKNER** ✓ +	**HUFF** R 45

R – REACHING

FT – FEET COMING TOGETHER, ETC.

Diagram 1-2. Mass Drill Chart

1. Since, as outlined earlier, all of our drills are of a competitive nature, the losing team has to run at the end of the drill. The winning team, however, would lose a considerable amount of practice time if it is allowed to simply stand around watching the other team run. Therefore, we instruct the winning team to do some sort of a shooting drill on the side baskets. Our favorite is a drill called "100 under-the-basket" (see

NAME / CRITERIA	GAME SHIRT		GAME SHORTS		LEGGINGS		WARM-UP PANTS		WARM-UP TOP		TRAVEL BAG	GAME SHOES	RED LACES
	3 Post moves	18 out of 20 FT's	Defending Double Post	Tiger Drill	Hawking the ball	Block-ing out	2-on-1 Off.	2-on-1 Def.	3-on-2 Off.	3-on-2 Def.	3-man Shell Drills	Give & Go / Screen & Roll / Screen Away / Weave	Split post / Double post / Single post / Zone pen.
SNEED	✓	✓	✓	✓			✓		✓		✓		✓
VRAZEL	✓	✓	✓	✓				✓		✓	✓	✓	
ALKEK	✓	✓		✓		✓		✓	✓		✓		
CONAWAY		✓	✓			✓		✓	✓		✓	✓	✓
BUCKNER	✓		✓		✓		✓		✓		✓		
ROSS	✓		✓			✓		✓		✓	✓		
WIMBISH	✓		✓			✓	✓		✓		✓	✓	✓
RUSSELL	✓		✓			✓		✓	✓		✓		

Diagram 1-3

Chapter 4). It is a short jumper drill, so there is little chance of a ball rolling out on the floor where the losing team is running.

2. It is easy to involve all of the players while doing drills. But during scrimmage sessions, unless there are only ten members of the team present, some will have idle time on their hands—unless the coach has planned an activity for those players. The best activity for these players would be some specially designed drill to improve each player's individual weakness. However, some coaches may prefer that the substitutes watch and listen to the instructions being given to players involved in the scrimmage. Also, these players could get involved by being referees, while at the same time learning the mechanics of this lucrative trade. By being directly involved, players tend to be more attentive to coaching instructions and learning situations as they present themselves during the scrimmage, not to mention the invaluable lessons learned from having to serve as an official. Players will not only learn to respect officials, but will gain greater insight as to the difficulty of positioning oneself properly to make correct calls.

Another suggestion to involve all players in a scrimmage situation is to have the substitutes dribble up and down the sidelines using the right hand going one way and the left hand going the other, and staying even with the ball. It's a good conditioning and dribbling drill if the coach can tolerate the added noise.

When using this technique, we have the players do silent ball-handling drills when the coach is giving instructions. This means that we use drills where the ball does not hit the floor, such as figure eights through the legs, around the waist, and ball movements around other parts of the body. If you want to teach your players to be able to shoot free throws without paying attention to noise distractions, have the sideline players "go wild"—screaming, dribbling, hollering, whistling, etc.—when the players involved in the scrimmage are at the free throw line.

3. Injured players can lose valuable time while recovering if a coach allows them just to sit and watch practice. With the trainer's approval, special workouts are designed and followed by our injured players. This helps not only to keep them in shape, but also to improve fundamental skills and player morale.

Below is an example of a workout for a player with an ankle injury. A manager is in charge of setting up equipment, timing, retrieving balls, and other duties that will help the rehabilitation of the injured athlete.

INJURED PLAYER WORKOUT

1.	Stretching exercises	5 min.
2.	Leg lifts—100 each leg Sit-ups—50 Fingertip push-ups (from knees)—50	5 min.
3.	Dribbling with right hand while sitting in chair—while squeezing a tennis ball with left—1 min.; left-hand dribble and right-hand squeeze—1 min. (Do 5 sets)	10 min.
4.	Wall volleyball: sitting in chair, hit volleyball against wall (both hands)—1 min.; right hand only—1 min.; left hand only—1 min. (Do 3 sets)	9 min.
5.	Passing medicine ball to manager while sitting: 10 chest passes, 10 overhead passes, 10 right-handed underhand passes, 10 left-handed underhand passes, 10 right-hand baseball passes, and 10 left-hand baseball passes. (Do 5 sets)	6 min.
6.	Lying flat on your back on a mat, shoot a basketball straight up into the air with one hand and catch it—25 right hand, 25 left hand, and 25 alternating. (Do 3 sets)	10 min.
7.	Shooting while sitting down: Use a basketball and shoot the ball into a large trash can set up on a table 10 feet away. (Make 100)	10 min.

Injured players are also expected to lift weights three days a week. We also have them listen to motivational tapes and work in a motivational workbook while they're engaged in ice and whirlpool treatments.

The injured player workouts are done during drill sessions, but during scrimmage sessions, players are expected to watch the workouts.

4. A practice which may seem absurd to some coaches is the timing of water breaks. We usually shoot free throws before a water break and then put two minutes on the clock. The clock buzzer is sounded every 15 seconds. Each player is allowed 15 seconds at the water fountain and is expected to come back on the floor and practice shooting for the remainder of the break. Although we employ the two-minute break, we do not necessarily enforce the 15-second limit at the fountain, unless we have problems with players abusing break privileges.

5. Another perhaps unusual custom is the fact that we practice the first day of school and the last day of school, and certainly every day in between. We do not waste several days going over rules and issuing

equipment at the beginning of school, and we don't take off early to check in equipment and take inventory. This means that coaches must work several days in advance to place equipment—such as shoes, socks, practice shorts, and shirts—into players' lockers, and that they must work into the summer to remove player equipment from lockers and do a final inventory report. We ask 100 percent from players, so as a coaching staff, we must be willing to give a little extra ourselves.

It may sound strange, but our players always seem proud to be the first athletic team to work out and the last to quit.

2 How to Draw Up—and Follow—A Blueprint For Success

When I was a young coach, I attended a coaching school lecture given by Dean Foshee, one of the "grand old masters" of girls' basketball in Texas at the time. He said, "In order to have a successful program, you must first have a philosophy." Although I did not realize the magnitude of his statement at the time, I made a resolution to do just that—develop a philosophy.

DEVELOPING YOUR OWN COACHING PHILOSOPHY

There are many approaches that can be used in developing a philosophy, but the one I favor is a simple question-and-answer process.

QUESTION	ANSWER
1. What is my goal?	1. To win the State Championship.
2. What must I do to accomplish this goal?	2. a) Teach sound fundamental skills. b) Have the best defense in the state. c) Be willing to fast break in a controlled manner every time. d) Dominate the offensive and defensive boards.

Each answer is a sub-goal and must undergo the same question-and-answer process. For example:

QUESTION	ANSWER
1. What must I do to have the best defense in the state?	1. Play a pressure, man-for-man defense.
2. What is a pressure, man-for-man defense?	2. It applies constant pressure on all opponents with or without the ball.
3. What must I do to accomplish this?	3. a) Teach players how to guard a player with the

ball inside and outside the
scoring area.

b) Teach players how to
guard a player without the
ball on the perimeter and
inside the post area.

4. What methods will I use to
teach these skills?

5. What drill would best teach
how to guard a player . . .
with the ball inside the scoring area?

6. . . . dribbling the ball outside
the scoring area?

7. . . . without the ball on the
perimeter?

8. . . . without the ball in the
post area?

9. How much time should be
devoted to these drills?

10. How can I make sure that
players are giving 100 percent
effort and executing stances
correctly?

4. Establish a series of situation-
reaction drills.

5. One-on-one from the free
throw line (see Chapter 5).

6. "Hawking-the-ball" full court
(see Chapter 5).

7. "Tiger" drill (see Chapter 5).

8. Defending the Double Post
Drill (see Chapter 5).

9. Five-min. drills every Monday, Wednesday, and Friday.

10. a) Make the drills competitive where losers have to
run (see Chapter 3).

b) Employ the "Earn Your
Uniform" system (see
Chapter 1).

ESTABLISHING AN EFFECTIVE WORKOUT SCHEDULE

Once you have developed your philosophy through the question-
and-answer process of each sub-goal, you are ready to write out a workout schedule which employs a systematic approach to achieving your
goals.

Although the workout schedules that we use in our program are
included here, they should simply serve as a guide in setting up your
own workout schedule. Each individual coach should have his or her
own unique philosophy that determines what drills he or she will use in
designing a practice format. For instance, the drill I call the "Tiger
Drill" teaches my players how to deny the pass to a perimeter player. If
your philosophy does not call for denying the pass to perimeter players,
it would be much more beneficial for you to replace this time slot with a

drill that teaches your players how far away to play from the perimeter player receiving the pass, or how to approach a perimeter player who has just received the ball.

These schedules should first be looked at as a whole in order to grasp the concept of a systematic workout schedule. Be careful, however, not to spend too much time studying each individual drill. The references as to where the description of each drill may be found in this book will serve you best when you actually prepare to write down your practice schedule. For example, you can find the description of a drill, such as "Hawking-the-ball" (see Chapter 6), and then say to yourself, "Well, we don't pressure the dribbler, so let me replace this time slot with a favorite drill of mine that teaches the shifts of a 2-3 zone." Each time slot can be replaced by a drill of your own (that will hopefully be made competitive after reading this book) until a systematic workout schedule has been designed to implement your own philosophy.

Now let us take a look at the workout schedule used in our program. The workout schedule which we use at all levels in our program—grades 7 through 12—during our 50-minute athletic period is as follows:

DRILL	TIME	SPECIAL STIPULATIONS
"Daily Form Shooting Drill" (see Chapter 4)	6 min.	Failure to put "hand in the basket" should be punished by push-ups, sprints, etc.
1-on-1 from the free throw line	5 min.	Losers run a horse under 45 sec. Individually, during the drill, if you don't score, run a lap or sprint; run a lap or sprint if they score on you. (Award baskets for excessive fouling or make them run 2 sprints, etc.). In case of a tie, both teams run. Failure to run from line to line, missing a turn, anything less than a 100 percent effort by anyone, griping at teammates, managers keeping score, etc., should result in everyone running an extra horse at the end of the drill. If it is excessive, stop the drill and run them right then to get the point across.

"Tiger" drill or Cover-Out	5 min.	(Same as above)
"Hawking-the-ball"	5 min.	(Same as above)
Defending the Double Post Drill	8 min.	(Same as above, except individuals do not run)
Blocking Out Drill	6 min.	(Same as above)
2-on-1 and 3-on-2 Full Court Drill (see Chapter 6)	10 min.	(Same as above as described in 1-on-1 from the free throw line, except the players do not have to run if they are scored on—unless the players aren't trying.)
Killer Drill (see Chapter 8)	1 min.	Losing team runs; the others go get dressed.

This is our defensive workout schedule. It is followed religiously on Monday, Wednesday, and Friday during the athletic period throughout the season. Days of games are no exception, except that the running for losing may be lessened.

Tuesday and Thursday are our offensive workout days. Early in the season, the offensive drills are practiced on Tuesday without the defense, as we are looking for proper execution. Later in the season, Tuesday as well as Thursday become competitive workout sessions, stressing basic offensive concepts used in all of our offensive sets.

TUESDAY (Non-competitive early in the season) and THURSDAY (Competitive):

DRILL	TIME	SPECIAL STIPULATIONS
1. "Daily Form Shooting Drill"	6 min.	Failure to put "hand-in-basket" should be punished by push-ups, sprints, etc.
2. 3-man Shell Drills done Tues. and Thurs. (see Chapter 12) a. Hi-lo action b. Pass opposite c. Post penetration d. Wing penetration	3-min. drills (1-1/2 min. from each side when non-competitive)	On non-competitive days, use the Mass Drill Charts to evaluate indiv. performance. We want the smallest of things done perfectly. You may employ "a goal for the day" method. On competitive days, have losers run, etc., as described in the defensive workout.

  e. Switch out
  f. Guard cut, fill
   and turn
  g. Triple post
   rotation

3. Tuesday 2-on-2 and 3-on-3 drills (see Chapter 7) a. Give and go b. Screen and roll c. Screen away d. Weave	3 min. drills	Losers run at the end of each 3-min. drill as described in the defensive workout.
4. Thursday 2-on-2 and 3-on-3 drills (see Chapter 7) a. Split-the-post b. Double post c. Single post d. Zone penetration	3 min. drills	Losers run at the end of each 3-min. drill as described in the defensive workout.
5. 2-on-1 and 3-on-2 Full Court Drill done Tues. and Thurs.	6 min. drill	(Same as above)

  This offensive workout schedule is followed religiously on Tuesday and Thursday during our athletic period throughout the season.

  Our after-school workouts are just as meticulously planned and rigidly followed. Our two-hour workout schedule is as follows:

ACTIVITY	TIME	ACCUMULATIVE
1. Warm-up: (Layups and special 1-4 options without defense)	4 min.	4 min.
2. Specialty things:		
a. Jump ball center play	1 min.	5 min.
b. Jump ball under play	1 min.	6 min.
c. Sideline play front court	1 min.	7 min.
d. Sideline play back court	1 min.	8 min.
e. Under-the-basket play	1 min.	9 min.
f. Preserving-a-lead inbounds play	1 min.	10 min.
g. 4-second play	1 min.	11 min.

h. Sideline fast break 2-on-1 (see Chapter 10)	2 min.	13 min.
i. Sideline fast break 3-on-2	2 min.	15 min.
3. Press breaker work (see Chapter 11):		
a. Dummy press breaker		
(1) 2-on-1	2 min.	17 min.
(2) 3-on-2	2 min.	19 min.
(3) 3-on-3 early offense (see Chapter 10)	2 min.	21 min.
b. Attacking a 100 press		
(1) on the ball press	3 min.	24 min.
(2) off the ball press	3 min.	27 min.
Free Throw Shooting and Water Break	2 min.	29 min.
c. Attacking a 75 press		
(1) even front press	3 min.	32 min.
(2) odd front press	3 min.	35 min.
d. Attacking a 50 press		
(1) even front press	2 min.	37 min.
(2) odd front press	2 min.	39 min.
4. Overtime and delay game work	15 min.	54 min.
Free Throw Shooting and Water Break	2 min.	56 min.
5. Attacking man and match-up defenses	15 min.	1 hr. & 11 min.
6. Attacking odd front zones	12 min.	1 hr. & 23 min.
7. Attacking even front zones	12 min.	1 hr. & 35 min.
Free Throw Shooting and Water Break	2 min.	1 hr. & 37 min.
8. Attacking 25 trapping zones	10 min.	1 hr. & 47 min.
9. Attacking the Box & 1 and the Triangle & 2	10 min.	1 hr. & 57 min.
10. Pressure free throw shooting	3 min.	2 hrs.

In Texas, high schools are not allowed to practice after school until October 15th, but they are allowed to practice up to one hour during an in-school athletic period. Therefore, we have pre-season workouts. These workouts are very structured. There is an emphasis on conditioning and fundamental skills with activities leading up to our Monday, Wednesday, Friday defensive workout schedules, and Tuesday, Thursday offensive workout schedules. The pre-season workout schedule is as follows:

MONDAY, AUGUST 27th:

Call attention to the rules and discipline sheets that need to be taken home for their parents to read and sign.

Organize mass drill formation and go over the following fundamental skills (10 minutes):

1. Position of hands on the ball
   a. shooting hand
   b. guide hand

2. Triple Threat Position
   a. High Post Moves—use both feet as pivot foot
      1) Jab, crossover, dribble
      2) Jab, rocker, shot
      3) Jab, lean and go

3. Pivoting—both feet
   a. Forward pivot
   b. Reverse pivot
   c. Emphasize moving the ball
   d. Emphasize pivot foot staying in one place—up on ball of foot and knees bent

4. Jump shot (see Chapter 4)
   a. Teach proper release of the ball—one-handed shot
   b. Triple threat and up
   c. Triple threat and shot

Circuit Training Stations (40 minutes):

1. Weights (10 min.)

2. Jumping circuit (10 min.)

3. Form shooting drills (6 min.) and free throw ritual (4 min.) (see Chapter 4)

4. Layup variations: Regular (2 min.), Power (2 min.), Power Slide (2 min.), Lay-backs (2 min.) and Crossover (2 min.) (see Chapter 4) (10 min. total)

TUESDAY, AUGUST 28th:

Fundamental skills taught in mass drill. Review the previous day's mass drill activities and go over the following dribbling variations:

1. exchange	5. crab
2. double exchange—right and left	6. stutter
3. half reverse—right and left	7. backward
4. full reverse	8. behind-the-back

Circuit Training Stations (45 minutes):

1. Colorado jump rope procedure (15 min.): Jump 30 sec. non-stop; rest for 15 sec. Each jumping interval increases by 30 sec., but the rest interval of 15 sec. remains the same. The longest non-stop jumping interval is 2 min. and 30 sec. Following this interval, the length of time of each jumping interval decreases by 30 sec. with the rest intervals remaining at 15 sec. each, until the last interval of 30 sec. is completed. It is a 14-1/2 min. routine.

2. Dribbling drills through chairs (10 min.) and ball handling drills (5 min.)—(15 min. total).

3. Form shooting drills (6 min.), free throw ritual (5 min.), and high post moves without the defense (4 min.)—(15 min. total).

WEDNESDAY, AUGUST 29th:

—Fundamental skills taught in mass drill. Review the previous day's activities and add the three basic post moves (see Chapter 4) and the correct passing form of the chest pass, two-hand overhead, baseball, bounce (2-handed and 1-handed), underhand or shovel and lob passes (10 min.).

—Circuit Training Stations (40 minutes): (Same as Monday, August 27th except add various types of passes to layup drills [see Chapter 3]).

THURSDAY, AUGUST 30th:

—Fundamental skills in mass drill. Review the previous day's activities (5 min.).

—Circuit Training Stations (45 minutes): (Same as Tuesday, August 28th).

FRIDAY, AUGUST 31st:

—Fundamental skills taught in mass drill. Review and add instruction for offensive and defensive rebounding (see Chapter 8) (10 min.).

—Circuit Training Stations (40 minutes): (Same as Wednesday, August 29th except add blocking out to form shooting drills. Explain that the defenders merely put their hands up to get their teammates used to shooting over a defender. They block out the shooter after the shot).

MONDAY, SEPTEMBER 3rd:

Labor Day

TUESDAY, SEPTEMBER 4th:

—Fundamental skills in mass drill. Review previous week's mass drill activities. Introduce defensive shuffles in mass drill (10 min.).
—Circuit Training Stations (40 minutes):

1. Weights (10 min.)
2. Jumping circuit (10 min.)
3. Form shooting drills (6 min.) and free throw shooting (4 min.)
4. Layup drills (5 min.) and low post in the box drill (see Chapter 4) (5 min.)

WEDNESDAY, SEPTEMBER 5th:

—Fundamental skills in mass drill. Review (5 min.).
—Circuit Training Stations (45 minutes):

1. Colorado jump rope procedure (15 min.)
2. Dribbling drills (5 min.), Ball handling drills (5 min.), and Hawking-the-ball drill (see Chapter 5) (5 min.)
3. Form shooting drills (6 min.), free throws (4 min.), 1-on-1 from the free throw line using high post moves (see Chapter 5) (5 min.)

THURSDAY, SEPTEMBER 6th:

—Fundamental skills in mass drill. Review (4 min.).
—Circuit Training Stations (40 minutes): (Same as Tuesday, September 4th).
—Introduce Killer Drill (see Chapter 8) (2 min.).

FRIDAY, SEPTEMBER 7th:

—Fundamental skills in mass drill. Review (4 min.).
—Circuit Training Stations (45 minutes): (Same as Wednesday, September 5th).
—Killer Drill (1 min.).

MONDAY, SEPTEMBER 10th:

— Fundamental skills in mass drill. Review (4 min.).
— Go over 2-on-1 points of execution (5 min.).
— Circuit Training Stations (40 minutes): (Same as Friday, September 7th except replace layup drills with a 2-on-1 drill [see Chapter 6]) (5 min.).
— Killer Drill (1 min.).

TUESDAY, SEPTEMBER 11th:

— Fundamental skills in mass drill. Review (4 min.).
— Circuit Training Stations (45 minutes):

   1. Colorado jump rope procedure (15 min.)

   2. Drilling and ball handling drills (5 min.), introduce Tiger drill (see Chapter 5) (5 min.), and Hawking-the-ball drill (5 min.)

   3. Form shooting drill (6 min.), free throws (4 min.), and 1-on-1 from the free throw line using high post moves (5 min.)

— Killer Drill (1 min.).

WEDNESDAY, SEPTEMBER 12th:

— Fundamental skills in mass drill. Review (4 min.).
— Introduce blocking out drill (see Chapter 8) and points of proper execution (5 min.).
— Circuit Training Stations (45 minutes): (Same as Monday, September 10th).
— Killer Drill (1 min.).

THURSDAY, SEPTEMBER 13th:

(Same as Tuesday, September 11th)

FRIDAY, SEPTEMBER 14th:

(Same as Wednesday, September 12th)

MONDAY, SEPTEMBER 17th:

— Form shooting drills (6 min.).
— Introduce 3-on-2 points of execution (see Chapter 6) (3 min.).
— Circuit Training Stations (40 minutes):

   1. Weights (10 min.)

2. Jumping circuit (10 min.)

3. 2-on-1 drill (5 min.), 3-on-2 drill (5 min.)

4. Outlet pass drill (see Chapter 8) (5 min.), blocking out drill (5 min.)

—Killer Drill (1 min.).

TUESDAY, SEPTEMBER 18th:

—Form shooting drills (5 min.).
—Circuit Training Stations (45 minutes):

1. Colorado jump rope procedure (15 min.)

2. Tiger drill (5 min.), Hawking-the-ball (5 min.), 1-on-1 from the free throw line (5 min.)

3. Introduce Defending the double post drill (see Chapter 5) (8 min.), Blocking out drill (6 min.), Killer drill (1 min.).

WEDNESDAY, SEPTEMBER 19th:

—Introduce shell drills to teach basic offensive concepts (see Chapter 12) (9 min.).
—Circuit Training Stations (40 minutes):

1. Weights (10 min.)

2. Jumping circuit (10 min.)

3. 2-on-1 drill (5 min.) and 3-on-2 drill (5 min.)

4. Outlet pass drill (3 min.), Shell drills (7 min.)

—Killer Drill (1 min.).

THURSDAY, SEPTEMBER 20th:

(Same as September 18th)

FRIDAY, SEPTEMBER 21st:

—Form shooting drill (6 min.).
—Review shell drill points of execution (3 min.).
(Remainder of workout same as Wednesday, September 19th.)

MONDAY, SEPTEMBER 24th:

—Form shooting drill (6 min.).

—Introduce give-and-go drill, and screen and roll concepts (see Chapter 7) (3 min.).

—Circuit Training Stations (40 minutes):

1. Weights (10 min.)

2. Jumping circuit (10 min.)

3. 2-on-1 and 3-on-2 drill (see Chapter 6) (10 min.)

4. Shell drills (5 min.), introduce give-and-go drill (2-1/2 min.), introduce screen and roll drill (2-1/2 min.)

—Killer Drill (1 min.).

TUESDAY, SEPTEMBER 25th:

(Same as September 18th)

WEDNESDAY, SEPTEMBER 26th:

—Form shooting drill (6 min.).

—Introduce screen away and weave concepts (see Chapter 7) (3 min.).

—Circuit Training Stations (40 minutes):

1. Weights (10 min.)

2. Jumping circuit (10 min.)

3. 2-on-1 and 3-on-2 drill (5 min.), introduce screen away drill (2-1/2 min.), introduce weave drill (2-1/2 min.)

—Killer Drill (1 min.).

THURSDAY, SEPTEMBER 27th:

(Same as September 18th)

FRIDAY, SEPTEMBER 28th:

—Form shooting drills (6 min.).

—Review give and go, screen and roll, screen away, and weave concepts (3 min.).

(Remainder of workout same as September 26th.)

MONDAY, OCTOBER 1st:

—2-on-1 and 3-on-2 drill (6 min.).

—Introduce split-the-post and double post concept (see Chapter 7) (3 min.).

—Circuit Training Stations (40 minutes):

1. Weights (10 min.)
2. Jumping circuit (10 min.)
3. Introduce split-the-post drill (2-1/2 min.), introduce double post drill (2-1/2 min.), screen away drill (2-1/2 min.), weave drill (2-1/2 min.)
4. Shell drills (5 min.), give and go drill (2-1/2 min.), screen and roll drill (2-1/2 min.)

—Killer Drill (1 min.).

TUESDAY, OCTOBER 2nd:

(Same as September 18th)

WEDNESDAY, OCTOBER 3rd:

—2-on-1 and 3-on-2 drill (6 min.).
—Introduce single post and zone penetration concepts (see Chapter 7) (3 min.).
(Remainder of workout same as October 1st except replace shell drills with a 2-1/2 min. single post drill and a 2-1/2 min. zone penetration drill.)

THURSDAY, OCTOBER 4th:

(Same as September 18th)

FRIDAY, OCTOBER 5th:

—Shell drills (5 min.).
—2-on-1 and 3-on-2 drill (5 min.).
(Remainder of workout same as October 3rd.)

MONDAY, OCTOBER 8th, WEDNESDAY, OCTOBER 10th, and FRIDAY, OCTOBER 12th:

(Same as October 5th)

TUESDAY, OCTOBER 9th and THURSDAY, OCTOBER 11th:

(Same as September 18th)

Our post-season workout schedule includes a six to nine-week (depending on how well we do in the play-offs and how long our season lasts) track unit. During our 50-minute athletic period, every girl in our program goes through a sprinter's or a middle distance runner's workout on a daily basis. We feel that participation in track improves basketball's most basic fundamental skills—the ability to run quickly, correctly and effortlessly; endurance, stamina and overall conditioning; and increases mental toughness and individual competitiveness.

The last six weeks of post-season workout are not "set in concrete" as are our other workout schedules. The coaching staff evaluates the "shortcomings" of the team's performance over the past season and develops a plan of action to strengthen the team's weak areas for the coming year.

The first week off the track is set aside for measuring individual skill levels in these areas: shooting, jumping ability, jumping reach, arm and shoulder strength, quickness and lateral movement, speed, dribbling, and ball handling. The players are ranked according to their skills test scores. This helps determine who has the potential to be a varsity player the following season. Once we have determined who our personnel will probably be for the upcoming season, we evaluate their strengths and weaknesses and establish a post-season workout schedule. An example of our post-season workout schedule is as follows:

MONDAY, WEDNESDAY, and FRIDAY:

— Form shooting drills (6 min.).
— Circuit Training Stations (40 minutes):

1. Weights (10 min.)

2. Jumping circuit (10 min.)

3. Dummy press assignment drill (5 min.) and 2-on-1 trapping drill (5 min.)

4. 3-on-3 trap and floater drill (5 min.) and 2-on-1 and 2-on-2 fast break drill (5 min.)
   (See Chapter 9 for drills to develop the press)

— Killer Drill ladder tourney (4 min.).

TUESDAY and THURSDAY:

— Form shooting drills (5 min.).
— Circuit Training Stations (45 minutes):

1. "Get tough drills" (see Chapter 5)

    a. Mat basketball (5 min.)
    b. German football (5 min.)
    c. Loose ball drill (5 min.)

2. 4-on-4 trap, floater, sideline drill (5 min.), 5-on-5 full court press drill (5 min.), and 5-on-5 half court press drill (5 min.)

3. 4-on-2 fast break drill (see Chapter 10) (5 min.), run and jump man press drill (see Chapter 10) (5 min.), and blocking out drill (5 min.)

MAKING A COMMITMENT TO A PLAN OF ACTION

It should be obvious from the above-described workout schedules that I put emphasis on three areas of the game—defense, the fast break, and rebounding. There is certainly more to the game of basketball than these three areas, but we operate on the theory that it is better to be a master of some, rather than a master of none. If you observe the teams that consistently go to the state tournament year after year, you will find without exception that each of them has a trademark—something they are known for, something they do better than anyone else. For example, in Texas, Dallas South Oak Cliff, Houston Yates and Sweeny are known for their zone presses; Victoria for their pressure man-for-man defense; Duncanville for an exceptional double post game; Hardin for the triple post game.

None of these teams are masters in all areas of the game. There just isn't enough time in a single season to teach it all, so one must choose. Once the coach has decided what his/her team's trademark should be, then a plan of action should be prepared and rigidly followed.

Selecting a Coaching System That Fits Your Philosophy

Coaches can argue endlessly about X's and O's—whether ball games are won by offense or defense; whether zones are better than man defenses; whether full court presses are more effective than half court presses; whether scrimmage work is more valuable than drill work, etc. The end result of these arguments is a good-natured classification of coaches. In Texas, I am classified as a defensive-minded drill coach—a description, which if one can overlook its narrowness, is totally agreeable with my philosophy.

Yes, I believe that defense wins ball games. In seven appearances of my teams in the state finals, the two championships that were won had scores of 46 to 45 and 43 to 41. The other five championship games had scores of 55 or greater by our opponents. One of our team goals is to hold our opponents under 40 points. Each time we achieve this goal during the season, we award our players with a star which is placed on the back of their warm-up jackets. Holding our opponents to less than 40 points a game is not easy, but it is achievable; and each time we were near achieving it in the state finals, we won!

I believe that pressure man-for-man defense is the best defense to use if you plan to be a contender for the state championship year after year. The teams in Texas that hold the record for "most times in the state tournament"—Canyon (4A) 11 times, Spearman (3A) 10 times, and Moulton (2A) 8 times—were all famous for their pressure man-for-man defenses.

As a young coach, I admired this type of defense, but did not understand it well enough to teach it. In the 1976 state tourney finals, my team was ahead by one point in overtime with four seconds left on the clock. The opponents had the ball out of bounds under our basket along the baseline, but near the corner as we had deflected the ball out of bounds. We were in a sagging man defense with one defender fronting the other team's best post man and my tallest defender behind her. They inbounded the ball to a wing player who, for a split second, fumbled the ball, causing my fronting defender to take a step toward the seemingly loose ball. Their wing player recovered the ball and passed it to the tall post player who sank a turnaround jumper on the buzzer over my defender's outstretched hands. It was a bitter lesson to be learned. I vowed that instant I would never play that passive of a defense again. I made it a point that day to begin learning pressure defense.

Yes, I have a greater interest in defense than offense. I never realized the extent of this preference until a coaching friend of mine, Marsha Porter from Conroe, came to one of my workouts. After practice, I asked, "Well, what did you think?" "I think you need to go hire yourself a good offensive coach," was her reply. Although it hurt my ego, I managed to ask what she meant. "It's just that you hardly ever notice what the offense is doing, but you are constantly correcting the defense." Being aware of this preference has helped me make a more conscious effort toward being a better offensive coach, but more importantly, it has made me realize that my area of interest should be emphasized as I would most enjoy making it my area of strength.

And yes, I prefer drill over scrimmage work simply because it suits my personality better. I like the discipline, organization, and repetition of drills. I like perfecting the parts and then putting them together to make a perfect whole.

You can easily see that my philosophy of coaching is derived from my personal observations, experience, interests, and preferences. So it should be with each individual coach. His or her philosophy should be as unique as he or she is. What works for one coach will not necessarily work for another. There is no one particular "right way" of doing things.

There are many successful coaches who spend 90 percent of their time in scrimmage situations, others who teach a multitude of presses and zone defenses, and still others who rely on their team's offensive prowess to outscore opponents; but one can be sure that they all have a system to develop their trademark.

The techniques outlined in this chapter are not intended to hand over a ready-made philosophy or workout schedule. A drill coach should use this chapter to serve as a guide in selecting drills which are beneficial to his or her philosophy of the game. A scrimmage coach may still apply the philosophy of competition to his or her scrimmage situations, as will be discussed in considerable length in Chapter 12.

3 Designing Competitive Drills to Encourage 100 Percent Effort During Practice

In developing competitive drills, the form below will prove to be very helpful.

DEVELOPING COMPETITIVE DRILLS

I. THE OBJECTIVE OR PURPOSE OF THE DRILL (What is it that you want to accomplish?):

II. THE NAME OF THE DRILL:

III. POINTS OF EXECUTION:

    A. Formation

    B. Rotation

    C. Description

IV. THE CHALLENGE (What do you have to do to win?):

V. SPECIAL STIPULATIONS AND/OR PENALTIES:

VI. THE REWARD FOR WINNING OR THE PENALTY FOR LOSING:

Let us examine each part closely.

How to Determine the Drills' Objectives

Drills obtain the best results when their objective or objectives are very specific. As stated in Chapter 2, a philosophy is a series of seemingly endless questions and answers which start with a broad statement of a goal or objective. This goal or objective is further narrowed down to sub-goals such as: "We want our team to fast break in a controlled manner." It is now up to the coach to select a method which will teach a controlled fast break. For the drill coach, he or she will probably select a series of progressive drills leading up to one favorite drill which encompasses all the points of execution of the lead-up drills.

For example, it is our philosophy to fast break after a missed field goal or free throw attempt and after a made free throw. After a made field goal, however, we feel that haste may cause a turnover against a "surprise" press. We also feel that we can best attack a press by running a controlled press breaker which employs our fast break principles (see Chapter 11). Our philosophy, therefore, dictates that the majority of our fast breaks begin with a rebound, so we use a progression of drills with specific objectives to lead up to our favorite fast break drill.

As you will notice in our pre-season workout schedule (see Chapter 2), the first rebounding drill we introduce and use throughout the year is a nonaggressive blocking-out drill that is incorporated into our daily form shooting drills. The objective of this drill is to teach players proper execution in blocking out the shooter. We are working strictly on making the mechanics of blocking out a habit.

Our players must execute according to the following instructions: You are between your man and the basket when the ball goes up, so watch the player you are guarding, not the flight of the ball. If the player makes a move toward the basket, you take one shuffle step to block her way and then reverse pivot in the direction she is going. This move will assure you that the player is behind you without unnecessary contact. You should bring your arms up shoulder high, elbows out, and hands toward the basket.

The next rebounding drill which is introduced in our pre-season workout is the Killer drill (see Chapter 8). One of the objectives of this drill is to teach aggressive rebounding. This is followed by the introduction of a blocking out drill whose objective is to teach blocking out correctly and aggressively, not only the shooter, but a perimeter player without the ball. The drill progresses to teaching how to block out the post players when the ball is shot from different spots on the floor (see Chapter 8).

The final blocking out drill leading up to the fast break is the outlet pass drill (see Chapter 8). The objective of this drill is to teach players how to outlet the ball on a rebound to initiate the fast break. Players execute according to the following instructions: The rebounder should turn in mid-air toward the sideline closest to her. Upon landing, the feet and, therefore, the body should be turned toward the outlet receiver. A straight arm, overhead pass with good "snapping" wrist action should be used to deliver the ball.

As you can see, each drill has a specific objective that has to be accomplished before the fast break can successfully be initiated from a missed shot. While mastering proper rebounding and outlet skills, other drills which teach lane assignments—getting the ball to the middle, etc.—are being taught in different drills in our workout schedule. Eventually a combination of all skills taught in these drills is merged into one drill, the 2-on-1 and 3-on-2 transition fast break drill. We feel this is the best drill to use daily in teaching the fast break according to our philosophy.

The goal or objective should be stated simply and explicitly so that it is meaningful to you and, depending on your situation, also to your coaching staff. It is also important that you state the objective to your players so they can understand how the skills they are learning in a particular drill will be used in a game situation.

Name of the Drill

Giving each drill a name is important if you are conscientious about using your practice time wisely. When the name of a drill is called out by the coach, the players should immediately run to their places on the floor to begin the drill at the sound of the whistle. If a coach must stop practice each time he or she wants to change the drill, valuable practice time is lost.

The name itself can be motivational, such as "Tiger" drill or "Blitz" drill, if you are inclined to be creative. This not being my strong suit, I usually prefer the name to be descriptive, such as "2-on-1 and 3-on-2" drill or "Defending the Double Post."

How to Map Out Points of Execution for Each Drill

As you prepare checklists for proper execution of fundamental skills during a particular drill for your players (see Chapter 1), you must also prepare for yourself a checklist of three logistic problems which must be resolved if a drill is to be performed efficiently.

The first logistic problem you must take into consideration is the formation of the drill. The most simple way to take care of this matter is to diagram the formation in the following fashion:

Formation (for 2-on-1 and 3-on-2 Transition drill). (See Diagram 3-1 on page 43.)

Having solved the problem of what formation to use, the rotation of players during the drill is the next problem to be resolved. Assuring proper rotation during the drill is a must for the time-conscious coach.

After diagramming the drill, number the lines. This is the key to fluid rotation. Make sure that the first player in each line knows how to rotate from line #1 to #2 to #3 and back to #1. Tell the rest of the players to follow the man in front of them.

The rotation of this drill is so simple that it may seem to be belaboring the point, but the formation and rotation of many drills in this book are quite complicated. If a system of rotation such as the one described above is not established, there will be constant confusion and bickering among the players.

Upon first introducing a drill, I sometimes use cones or chairs with numbers on them to mark player lines to facilitate their rotation. Another helpful hint for fluid rotation is to enforce the rule that if a line is empty, somebody takes it, and the players should try to straighten out the rotation the best they can as the drill continues. Players should never stop the drill unless signaled by the coach.

The final logistic problem to be considered is the description of the drill. The description should be brief and to the point, and stated in the simplest manner possible in order to save time and avoid confusion. The following is a description of our 2-on-1 and 3-on-2 transition drill as it is given the first day that the drill is introduced:

The red team starts off with the ball. They go down the court and play 2-on-1 against the lone defender of the blue team. When the blue team gains possession of the ball by a steal or a rebound or after a made basket, they will go down the court trying to score on a 3-on-2 situation against X_1 and X_2.

After the initial introduction of this drill, the coach gives the description in a much shortened form: "Okay, 2-on-1 and 3-on-2 drill. Blue will be shooting at this basket (pointing toward a particular goal), and red will be shooting at that basket (pointing toward the opposite goal)."

As the players quickly move into the proper formation, the coach shouts out: "Red will start with the ball and go 2-on-1. Remember, one pass only on a 2-on-1 and two passes on a 3-on-2. If you don't score, you have to run a lap before rotating. Losers will have to run a horse." The coach blows the whistle and the drill begins.

The last part of the description had to do with the challenge and the special stipulations of the drill. The challenge and special stipulations deal with player motivation and emphasis on execution. The detailed discussions which follow will help clarify their importance.

The Challenge: What Players Must Do in Order to "Win" the Drill

The challenge should state what criteria must be met to keep from running at the end of the drill. In the above-described 2-on-1 and 3-on-2 drill, the team scoring the most baskets does not have to run.

There are countless ways to state the challenge, depending on what it is you want to accomplish. Most of our shooting drills require our players to beat the clock. For instance, we might require a team to make 25 layups in one minute.

An emphasis on a particular skill may be included in the challenge. If we are, perhaps, stressing blocking out, we may only award points, in a particular drill, for defensive rebounds. If we are concentrating on offensive rebounds, we may award three points instead of the customary two for every offensive rebound put back up and made.

Our concentration may be on making a certain number in a row. One of our free throw drills calls for this method. Two minutes are put on the clock. Players are paired off at each basket. Only one player shoots while the other rebounds. The player at the line has to try to make three free throws in a row. The rebounder counts how many times the shooter accomplishes this in the allotted time. After two minutes, they change roles and she must now try to beat the number of times that the other player made three in a row. At the end of the drill, the loser runs five sprints while the winner practices shooting or ball handling, or occasionally a water break is given as a reward.

How to Set Up Special Stipulations or Penalties

Special stipulations, generally, deal with points of execution that are being emphasized, such as those described in the 2-on-1 and 3-on-2 drills. Our philosophy is that you have time for only one pass on a 2-on-1 situation and two passes on a 3-on-2 before the opponents recover and come breathing down your neck. Thus, we allow only that number of passes in all of our 2-on-1 and 3-on-2 drills.

Special stipulations also deal with our immediate reward or punishment philosophy. If you don't produce, you have to run. For instance, if you don't score in our 2-on-1 and 3-on-2 drills as previously described, you have to run a lap before rotating to your next line. If you miss a layup, you may have to do ten push-ups before moving to the rebound line. In our free throw drills, if you miss two in a row, you have to sprint to the other end of the gym and back before you may resume shooting.

Special stipulations may simply emphasize attainment of a higher skill level. For example, in our free throw shooting drills, we may count only those free throws which are all net and do not touch the rim. In our rebounding drills, we may count only tip-ins. In our dribbling and defensive full court drills, we may allow the offensive player to use only the behind-the-back dribble. On our inbounds and outlet drills, we may allow only left-handed baseball passes.

In summary of the role that these special stipulations play in our program, we feel that they motivate athletes to concentrate on mastering the smallest points of execution. Unless you have a team with superior natural ability, the small details of execution will be the most critical element for the success of your team. The small points of execution must be included in your drills or you will gain little more than conditioning from the drills which are described in this book.

In stressing the importance of proper execution, I often remind my players that the drills we use are not any different than the drills used by teams all over the state, the nation, or the world, for that matter. Everybody uses 2-on-1 and 3-on-2 drills to improve their fast break. The reason ours is more effective is the fact that we execute better than anyone else. That is why all drills must be executed according to the explicit instructions that are given.

The Reward for Winning—the Penalty for Losing

A list of the rewards for winning and the punishments for losing is endless. A few of our favorites will be explained to serve as a guide for developing your own system.

Rewards

Instead of having to run, winners are rewarded in the following ways:

1. *100 Under-the-Basket* (see Chapter 4)—While the losing team is running, the winning team will go through an easy shooting drill. This particular drill, which will be described in further detail in Chapter 4, is our favorite shooting drill to use during our athletic period workout when the gym is very crowded. The drill uses minimal floor space, rarely creates a loose ball situation which could cause a safety hazard for players running on the main floor, yet provides adequate time in practicing a fundamental skill which is so often overlooked—under-the-basket shooting.

2. *Ball Handling Drills*—Ball handling drills can be performed by the winning team while the losers are running, but they take up more floor space. And with each player handling a basketball, the chances of a loose ball rolling out on the floor where the other players are running are greatly increased—thus creating a safety hazard.

3. *Water Breaks*—Occasionally we allow the winning team to take a water break while the other players are running.

4. *Go in Early*—If the drill is the last drill of the day, we usually allow the winning team to go in while the losing team runs.

5. *Picture on the Bulletin Board*—On Monday of each week, managers are assigned to the various baskets in the gym to tally the number of baskets scored on each individual player. The player allowing the least number of baskets is named the Defensive Player of the Week. On Tuesday of each week, managers tally the number of baskets that each player makes during the athletic period. The player scoring the most

baskets is named the Offensive Player of the Week. The players' pictures are pinned up on the bulletin board.

6. *Player of the Week*—On Friday of each week, a player from the Varsity, Junior Varsity, and Freshman team is named Player of the Week. This is awarded by the coaching staff for outstanding performance in all workouts during the week. The players get to wear a special workout shirt imprinted with Player of the Week during all practice sessions in the upcoming week.

Punishments

Losing is always followed by some sort of punishment which usually consists of some sort of running. A clock is used to time the punishment. If anyone in the group fails to beat the clock, the entire group has to run again. Several seconds are usually added, as the group will be somewhat fatigued from the prior attempt.

The following is a description of the punishments we use most frequently:

1. *Forward Horse*—Players line up side by side along one baseline. Forty to forty-five seconds are put on the clock. When the coach blows the whistle, the players run in a straight line and touch with their foot the free throw line or an imaginary extension of the free throw line. They sprint back to the original baseline and touch it with a foot and then turn and sprint to the mid-court line, touch it with their foot and then sprint back to the original baseline. After touching the baseline with a foot, they turn and sprint to the far free throw line (or free throw line extended), touch it with their foot and then sprint back to the original baseline. Having contacted the original baseline with a foot, the players turn and sprint to the far baseline, touch it with a foot and then sprint to the original baseline. From the original baseline, players sprint to the far baseline to end the regimen.

It should be noted that in the above description players are required to touch lines with their foot. Sometimes we ask our players to touch the lines with their hand or hands, or even a basketball if players are dribbling. This requirement will be excluded in the remaining description for sake of brevity.

2. *Forward-Backward Horse*—The procedure is the same as for the Forward Horse except that the players return to the original baseline each time by running backwards. Forty to forty-five seconds should be sufficient time for the group to complete this regimen.

3. *Forward, Backward, Hop and Bound Sprints*—Players line up side by side along one baseline. One minute is put on the clock. When the coach blows the whistle, the players run in a straight line to the free throw line (or free throw line extended). They quickly turn and run backward to the mid-court line where they quickly turn and hop to the

free throw line (or free throw line extended) farthest from the original baseline. Upon reaching this line, the players run forward without bending their knees (which we refer to as bounding) to the far baseline. Upon reaching the baseline, the players quickly turn and follow the same procedure of forward running, backward running, hopping and bounding to return to the original baseline. Each time a baseline is touched, whether it be the original or far baseline, it is counted as one sprint. Seven sprints should be completed in one minute.

4. *Shuffle, Backward, Shuffle, Forward Sprints*—Players line up side by side along one baseline. One minute is put on the clock. When the coach blows the whistle, the players, facing the coach who is positioned along one sideline, shuffle to the nearest free throw line or free throw line extended. Upon reaching this line, they quickly turn and run backward to the mid-court line where they quickly turn so that their backs are to the coach, and then proceed to shuffle to the free throw line or free throw line extended farthest from the original baseline. Upon reaching this line, the players quickly turn and run forward to the far baseline. Upon reaching the baseline, the players quickly turn to face the coach and shuffle to the nearest free throw line to follow the same procedure of shuffling, backward running, shuffling and forward running to return to the original baseline. Each time a baseline is touched, it is counted as one sprint. Five to six sprints should be completed in one minute.

5. *Forward Suicides*—Players line up side by side along one baseline. Thirty to thirty-five seconds are put on the clock. When the coach blows the whistle, the players run forward to the opposite baseline and then quickly return to the original baseline. Upon reaching the original baseline, they quickly run to the far free throw line (or extension, thereof) and once again return to the original baseline. They quickly sprint to the mid-court line and return to the original baseline and then sprint to the closest free throw line (or free throw line extended), and then make a quick dash to the original baseline to end the regimen.

6. *Forward-Backward Suicide*—The procedure is the same as for the Forward Suicide except that players return to the original baseline each time by running backwards. Thirty to thirty-five seconds should be adequate time for the group to complete the regimen.

7. *Dribbling Horse or Dribbling Suicide*—The procedure is the same as for the Forward Horse or Forward Suicide except that the players are dribbling a basketball. They are instructed to dribble with their right hand going one way and with their left hand going the other. The time may remain the same or be adjusted according to the skill level.

8. *Shuffling or Crab Dribble Horse*—The procedure is similar to a suicide or horse while dribbling except that using this dribble, the crab

dribble, the player, as she shuffles, dribbles the basketball right between her knees with her right hand if her left foot is the lead foot of the shuffle, and left hand if the right is the lead foot of the shuffle. One minute is put on the clock. Players lined up along the baseline shuffle and dribble simultaneously, crab dribble, to the opposite baseline and back to the original baseline and then to mid-court and back to the original baseline. As our program is defensive-oriented, we emphasize a wide stance while shuffling and are more concerned with proper form than speed. If you are concerned with speed, a complete suicide could be finished in one minute.

9. *Half a Horse*—Players line up side by side along one sideline. Twelve seconds are put on the clock. When the coach blows the whistle, the players run to an imaginary line extending the length of the court from one basket to another dividing the court in half lengthwise. They quickly turn and run back to the original sideline and then sprint to the far sideline and back to the original starting line.

10. *One Lap*—Players line up along one sideline one behind the other. Eighteen seconds are put on the clock. When the coach blows the whistle, the players run around the boundary lines of the basketball court and return to their original starting spot before the buzzer sounds.

Individual Regimens

The above-described running regimens are used when running an entire team for losing a competitive drill, scrimmage, etc. As stated in the previous chapters, players often must run after immediate failure during the drills. For instance, in our one-on-one drills, if a player you are guarding scores on you, you must run a bleacher, run a sprint, touch your heels ten times, or crab walk to mid-court and back before rotating to your next assignment line. A description of these individual regimens is as follows:

1. *Run a bleacher*—The individual player must run up the bleachers and touch the video or camera platform in the uppermost middle section of the bleachers and then walk down. This takes 15 to 20 seconds.

2. *One sprint there and back*—Players run and touch the opposite gym wall and run back. This requires 10 to 12 seconds.

3. *Heel touch ten times*—Player jumps up bending her knees so that her feet come up in back of her nearly as high as her buttocks. She touches her heels with her hands which are in back of her. She does this 10 times which requires about 8 seconds.

4. *Crab walk to mid-court and back*—Players sit down on the floor with their hands resting on the floor behind them. Their feet are in front

of them with the knees bent at about a 90-degree angle. They raise their buttocks off of the ground and walk on their hands and heels of their feet, without their buttocks touching the floor, to the mid-court line and back. This takes 15 to 20 seconds.

SPECIAL CONSIDERATIONS FOR USING COMPETITIVE DRILLS MOST EFFECTIVELY

One of the biggest complaints I hear from coaches who have adopted my system of competitive drilling is the fact that there is an increase in anger flareups among team members. This is quite natural as players are pitted against each other in a win or lose situation on a daily basis. The positive side of this is the fact that it is one of the first signs of the desire to compete. However, the anger needs to be channeled into positive actions. This can best be accomplished by never allowing any outward display of negative emotion. We tell our players that if they can control the muscles of their bodies so that their elbow is in perfect alignment every time they take a shot, so that they execute a perfect reverse pivot every time they block out, so that they refrain from reaching out and "clothes-lining" someone driving past them, or in other words, so that they exhibit perfect muscular control playing the game, then they are equally capable of controlling any display of anger whether it be as grandiose as swinging a fist or whether it be a small facial grimace. All displays of anger are dealt with immediately.

On the first offense, I talk to the group as a whole about how spectators are turned off by outward displays of anger, how referees might get it in for a team because one player showed anger, how a technical foul in a crucial moment could cause us a state championship, and perhaps most importantly, how an untimely display of anger could cause the individual to not receive an honor such as all-state, or worse yet, a scholarship should a sportswriter or college coach be seated in the crowd and offended by the display.

On the second offense, I single out the individual and give the group a warning that everyone will have to run should another outburst be observed. On the third offense, everyone runs. Should we continue to have problems with an individual not being able to control her anger, she would be warned and dismissed from the team on the next offense. There is no room for a "time bomb" on a championship team.

Other problems such as cheating, poor effort, improper rotation, etc., are handled the same way. If a player does not have enough integrity to pull her share of the load in practice, then we can expect the individual not to have the integrity to be a team player. That player is more worried about herself than her teammates and must either change her behavior or be dismissed from the team. And if a player is not smart enough to remember the rotation order of the drills, she will never master our 5-on-5 offensive patterns and defensive assignments. If the brand of basketball is going to be of championship quality, the importance of the mental part of the game cannot be overlooked.

Positive Actions That Will Encourage Proper On-Court Behavior

It is the coach's responsibility to make every effort to alter players' undesirable behavior patterns. Some positive actions which can encourage proper on-court behavior and replace negative displays are as follows:

1. *Shaking hands*—A quick handshake with the fellow that you would like to "punch out" beats "counting to ten" in the game of basketball.

2. *Clapping your hands*—If you can't bring yourself to shake her hand, clap your hands together as if you were applauding. Keep on clapping until the anger passes—just as if you were counting to ten. If you succeed in defeating your anger, you deserve the applause.

3. *Suggestion box*—We have a suggestion box in the hallway by our dressing room. Players are encouraged to put unsigned notes in the box discussing any problem which the coach may need to know about. We encourage players who are having problems controlling their tempers to try to put down in writing what it is that is making them angry. The coach may be unaware of unnecessary roughness, cheating, or unsportsmanlike behavior of team members which may be inciting the problem. Just getting it off your chest sometimes helps.

Why Players Cheat—And How to Deter It

Regardless of the players' upbringing or dedication to the game of basketball, the temptation to cheat increases as the competition stiffens and the workouts become more grueling. As a coach, you can expect players of the highest character to cheat if they are not closely supervised. Some of the most common ways players will cheat during competitive drills are as follows:

1. *Wipe out*—A player who is going to get beat in a one-on-one drill may be tempted to wipe out the offensive player so she will not have to run.

2. *Missing a turn*—Some players will refuse to take their turn against the best player on the team, knowing they will get beat and probably have to run.

3. *Not running after you have failed to score or have been scored*

on—Many players will try to get out of running if the coach's back is turned or if they feel they were fouled.

Close supervision of the activities is a must if the coach plans to use competitive drills on a daily basis. Some helpful hints to deterring the above-described problems are as follows:

1. Award the team whose player got wiped out five points during the competition. Make the player who committed the wipe out do some sort of extra running at the end of the period, or take her out of the drill and just have her run for the remainder of the drill or the entire practice if necessary.

2. Have the player missing the turn play one on one against the best player on the team for five minutes after the practice, with the loser having to run a horse for every point they get beaten. You will probably have to do this only once. Word gets around.

3. Players caught cheating on the individual running drills cause their team's score to be put back to zero and they will have to run five horses after practice.

A frequent criticism of my program is my method of continually penalizing the loser. Some will argue that constantly focusing on punishment for losing will create an atmosphere for arguing, fighting, cheating and lying to eliminate the subsequent penalty for the loss. It is the opinion of some that the emphasis on competition should be spread equally between rewarding the victors as well as punishing the losers. They say it will provide a positive influence and help to motivate players for future effort. It will also help reduce the potential for team tension created by continually penalizing the losers. They suggest possibilities such as allowing the winners to rest, take an additional water break, sit during scrimmage periods, run less than specified, or leave a few minutes early. This, they feel, may be more advantageous than making the losers always run.

In my opinion, as to how evenly one should reward the winners and punish the losers, it should be left to the discretion of the coach after assessing the personality of his/her team. If they are a determined and dedicated group with a "whatever it takes" mentality, then constantly punishing the loser will probably be acceptable. This group will look upon it as an opportunity to improve their conditioning and have the feeling of self-satisfaction that they are using every second of practice time in a positive way. If they are a group with a "I'm not so sure this is worth it" mentality, they will probably be receptive to methods that reward good performances. They will not feel cheated of valuable practice time if they are given a water break or an extra rest period or dismissed from practice early. They will view it as their just reward for a good practice. Convincing the coach, who is as "driven" as I am to uti-

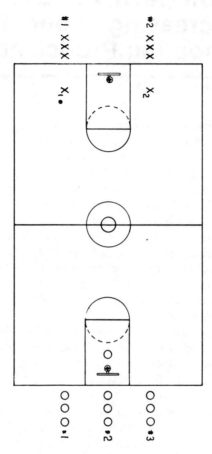

Diagram 3-1

lize fully each practice session, that the loss of practice time rewarding the athlete is well spent, would be a challenging task.

Designing competitive drills to get 100 percent effort from your players requires a lot of preparation and supervision by the coach. It takes a commitment to developing a philosophy, setting goals, designing drills, and developing workout schedules to achieve these goals. The work may be arduous, but the first championship will make it all worthwhile.

4 Competitive Drills For Increasing Your Players' Shooting Proficiency

It does not take an expert to recognize that the most glamorous fundamental skill of the game of basketball is shooting. Yet only a relatively small number of players become great shooters. There are many arguments as to what factors contribute to shooting proficiency. Some of the most popular ones are: "Stars are born, not made!" "He/she has an eye for the bucket!" "He/she simply spends every waking moment on the court shooting." "He/she has perfect form."

As a coach of many outstanding shooters, I have never resolved the question to my satisfaction. Some players spent hours practicing; some never worked on it outside of the scheduled practice that I demanded. Some had great jumping ability and strong wrist action; others were of extremely small stature and limited jumping ability. Some had good form; others were unorthodox.

From all of my observations and experiences, however, has developed a tenet by which I live and die. I insist that each individual in our program shoot the ball the same way. I don't tolerate what to me are unorthodox shooting styles from players who have been in our program since junior high. Occasionally, however, someone joins our program from another school. If we find her to be shooting with a great deal of success, we allow her to continue to use that shooting form, unless she is a Freshman or Sophomore. We change all of those who enter our program right away.

My first year at Victoria High School, I had the good luck of inheriting three excellent shooters—two with what I call sound shooting fundamentals; one with an unorthodox form (both elbows were out). This player held the ball directly above her head, and delivered it with two hands and very little wrist action. Unusual as it may sound, the shot was amazingly accurate. This young lady was averaging close to 20 points a game.

With only two district games left to play, however, an unusual thing happened. Something went awry with her shot, and she began shooting an extremely low percentage, scoring only six to eight points per game. By the time we played in the state finals, she was no longer in the starting lineup. From a player who had been vying for the team's top scoring honors to an unsteady reserve was the end result of an unorthodox shooting style. Although we spent hours analyzing what she was doing wrong on her shot, I felt helpless because I simply did not understand the mechanics that had made it go in in the first place.

I emphasize to my players that one of the main reasons for using the shooting form taught in our program is to enable me to help them should they start missing. Missed shots are the result of a misuse in execution of the mechanics of shooting. If they are not using the mechanics that we teach in our program, I cannot really help them. It's kind of like taking a radio that was bought at Sears to the J. C. Penny repair shop. They will tell you that they can't fix it because they don't know how it was put together in the first place. Jump shots, free throws, layups, etc., can be put together about as many ways as radios, cars, vacuum cleaners, watches, etc., but should they stop working, who will repair them?

DAILY "SHOOTING FORM" DRILLS

The first six minutes of our athletic period workout is devoted to teaching the correct shooting form. Our players learn to shoot over the rim first. For our starting one-minute shooting form drill (called the "one-handed shoot"), our players line up along the side of the basket (see Diagram 4-1). As previously discussed in Chapter 3, the first player in the line stands there facing the shooter with his arms extended straight up. The purpose of this player is two-fold. It gives the defensive player the opportunity to practice her blocking out form in a non-contact situation, enabling her to concentrate totally on form. It gives the offensive player someone to shoot over. The offensive player must learn to become oblivious of the defender. Her sole concentration should be on "pinpointing" the basket and using correct shooting form in releasing the ball. We teach the shot from what is called the "triple threat" position, so therefore it is included in the shooting instruction sheet that we give our players.

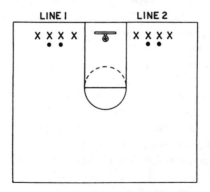

Diagram 4-1. One-Handed Shoot

Shooting Instruction Sheet

How do you hold a basketball? This may seem like a foolish question to you; but let's say that you are moving along the baseline and someone passes you the ball. What do you do with it?

The position that you hold the ball is called the "triple threat" position. From this position, you are a threat to pass the ball, dribble the ball, or shoot the ball.

The position of your hands on the ball and the stance you take are very important. Hold the ball in your hands so that the seams run across. Place the index finger of your shooting hand on one of the seams in the middle of the ball. Spread your fingers comfortably apart, so that the pads of your fingertips are resting on the ball. Spread your thumb so that the palm is raised slightly off the ball. You now have the proper position of your shooting hand on the ball.

Take your other hand, which we will refer to as the guide hand, and place your thumb on that part of the ball where the seams come together.

Your hands are now properly placed on the ball. Bring the ball up shoulder high. This is where the ball will be held if there is no pressure on the ball. If a defensive player is applying pressure, hold the ball at the level of the hip. Spread your feet comfortably apart, bend your knees for balance so that you are ready to move in any direction. You are now in what is referred to as the "triple threat" position.

Now bring the ball above your head to what is called the shooting position. You are ready to learn the most important fundamental in the game of basketball, and that is the proper release of the basketball when shooting. Make sure that your elbow is "in." This means that your elbow is in a straight line with your shoulder and your knee—not sticking out. This is very important in making sure that your shot will go in a straight line.

You should be holding the ball higher than your head, but in front of it. Your arm should form a 90-degree angle at the elbow. If there is a greater bend in your elbow, this will cause you to sling the ball at the basket instead of shooting it. Your wrist is cocked back to keep the ball from falling off of your hand. Your fingers should be comfortably apart, but remember that the palm of your hand does not make contact with the ball. The ball should rest only on your fingertips. This allows you to shoot with fingertip control.

Your feet should be comfortably apart and shoulders

should be square with the basket. Bend your knees. The ball stays above your head in shooting position. Bend your knees. Be careful not to bring the ball down as you bend your knees. The ball stays above your head in shooting position. Bend your knees slightly. As you begin to straighten your knees, shoot your arm straight up and break your wrist to shoot the ball. Stretch to shoot the ball. Raise up naturally on your toes and reach with your hand.

The ball should be released with your fingertips, and the action of your wrist breaking should give the ball a backward spin. This breaking of your wrist and stretching, reaching action of your body is referred to as the follow through. Your fingertips should point to the basket and remain there until the ball goes through the basket.

If you are releasing the ball properly, the ball will have a perfect "back spin." If the seams of the ball have an irregular spin, this means that you are not releasing the ball properly. You need to check the spin of the ball on your release. You might put white tape on the seams of the ball to magnify your back spin.

If you are just beginning to learn how to shoot, you should practice this one-handed shot straight into the air at least 100 times a day.

With all of these instructions in mind, the shooter assumes what we call "ready position." That is, she puts the ball above, but in front of her head, and takes her guide hand off of it. The guide hand remains up in the same plane of the ball to keep the shoulders square to the basket, but it is no longer in contact with the ball. The purpose of this drill is to concentrate on a one-handed release.

Having assumed "ready position," the players should be looking under the ball at a point on the rim nearest them. They should try to imagine what flight the ball will have to take so that it will go into the basket. They want to shoot the ball over the part of the rim nearest them. They should shoot the ball with a high arch, so that it hovers above the rim and then falls in.

As the shot is practiced, players should remember that the movement of the body and arm is straight up to give the ball the proper height. As the wrist breaks, the fingers will send the ball toward the basket. They should stretch their bodies as they pretend to reach for the rim with their fingertips. They must concentrate on their follow-through. Their arm should remain straight. Their wrist is flexed with their fingers pointing toward the basket. We ask them to exaggerate their follow-through by remaining in this reaching position until the ball goes through the basket.

The players rotate from line one to line two, becoming the rebounder after they have been the shooter. After rebounding, they take the ball with them to give it to the next shooter in the line they are rotating to.

The drill can also be done in competition, by having managers stationed at each basket keeping a tally of the number of baskets made. At the end of each one-minute segment, we have the losing teams do ten heel touches (see Chapter 3). Or we wait until all six one-minute drills have been completed to determine the winner and then have the losing teams run.

We post a "Goal for the Day" on the bulletin board prior to practice. Some of our favorites are: "Keep your elbows in." "Keep your shoulders square to the basket." "Make sure the ball is higher than, but is in front of, your head." "Make sure the ball is resting on your fingertips, not the palm of your hand." "Follow through until the ball goes through the basket." Should any player at a particular basket be caught not properly executing the "Goal for the Day," all of the players at that basket will have to run a horse at the end of the practice.

The Triple Threat Drill

The next one-minute shooting form drill that we do is called "Triple Threat." The players remain in the same formation with the same rotation and stipulations for running. This time they assume the triple threat position. One time they hold the ball shoulder high, pretending there is no defensive pressure; the next time they hold it on the hip, making believe that there is defensive pressure on the ball. The player jabs toward the basket with the foot closest to the baseline. Then she crosses over bringing the ball high over her head, dribbles once between her knees, squares to the basket, and shoots the ball. It is evident that the purpose of this drill is not as simple as that of the one-handed shoot. It is designed to teach the following fundamentals:

1. the "triple threat" position with or without pressure;

2. the jab, crossover offensive move;

3. protecting the dribble with one's body;

4. square to the basket;

5. proper shooting form of the jump shot;

6. proper rebounding form when the player is on defense.

Off the Pass and Up Drills

The next one-minute shooting drill is called "off the pass and up." The players form two lines at mid-court. The first player of each line takes her place at the wing position free throw line extended (see Dia-

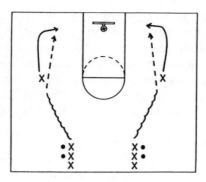

Diagram 4-2. Off the Pass and Up

gram 4-2). As the player with the ball dribbles toward her, the wing player floats toward the baseline. When the dribbler reaches the free throw line, she passes the wing player the ball. As the pass is in the air, the wing player takes a "giant step" toward the basket, so that she is ready to shoot the ball as soon as she receives the pass. According to our philosophy, the purpose of the drill is that it teaches players the following:

1. to position themselves free throw line extended as is the requirement of most of our offensive sets;

2. to float toward the baseline when the dribbler approaches their spot assignment;

3. to shoot the ball more quickly by taking the "giant step" toward the basket, which will automatically square them to the basket for the shot; and

4. the proper shooting form of the jump shot.

The players rotate from line one to line two. The stipulations for running remain the same.

Low Post Play Drills

The next three one-minute drills have to do with low post play. It is our philosophy that if our players can master three low post moves, they will score every time they receive the ball. The first priority of teaching post play is to teach the proper stance, which we refer to as posting up. To post up properly, we ask our players to stay low by bending their knees, and to stay wide by spreading their feet shoulder-width apart. Their upper arms are extended outward shoulder heighth, and their elbows bent at a 90-degree angle with the palms facing the passer. The stance is identical to that of the defensive rebounder.

Just as the rebounder's job is to keep the offensive rebounder behind her, the post player's primary objective is to keep the defensive player behind her. It is our philosophy that with the defensive player behind us, our post players can score every time. Post players must be willing to keep their feet moving constantly to keep their defender behind them. They must keep their back muscles taut between their shoulder blades. This makes the arms less flexible, and thus helps keep the defensive player from reaching around the post player to deflect a pass.

Once the stance has been established, the post player needs some direction as to where she is to establish or position herself. We tell our post players that the low post area is no wider than three feet on each side of the lane and no higher than ten feet up the key (see Diagram 4-3). Therefore we ask them to straddle the first hash mark above the square on either side of the key. This gives them enough maneuverability to "jockey" (battle the defensive player) for position and still have a good shooting angle should they choose to "power" to the basket.

The *first* one-minute post shooting drill is called "power to the baseline." The formation to the drill is as follows:

1. An offensive player positions herself on each side of the lane straddling the designated hash mark,

2. A defensive player assumes a cover-out stance from the lane side, thus taking the middle away,

3. A passer's line is set up on each side of the free throw line extended. The first player in this line who is the passer is instructed to line herself up in a straight line with the offensive post player (see Diagram 4-4).

From the triple threat position, the wing player passes in the ball to the post player who executes the "power to the baseline" move according to the following directions:

1. Upon receiving the pass, put the ball under your chin.

2. Keep your elbows out to protect the ball.

3. Look over your shoulder toward the middle of the key.

4. Upon seeing the defender taking away the middle, "drop step" (backward step toward the basket) your foot closest to the baseline, thus pinning your defender on your hip.

5. Put the ball right between your knees dribbling once to keep from traveling.

6. Square to the basket and put the shot up, being careful to keep the ball in front of your head to avoid it being blocked from behind.

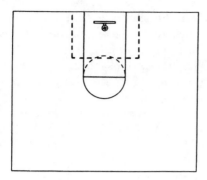

Diagram 4-3. Low Post Area

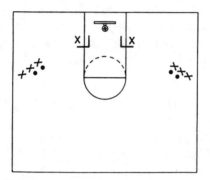

Diagram 4-4. Post Shooting Drill Formation

Later in the player's development, a pump fake may be added to the "power to the baseline" move. The player executes the same move, but instead of releasing the ball, she keeps her knees bent and merely straightens her arms to show the ball to the defensive player. The sight of the ball will usually make the avid "shot blocker" leave her feet. As the defensive player reaches the heighth of her jump, the offensive player leaves the floor to put the shot up. The defensive player on the way down from her jump is helpless, so the offensive player must be patient in timing this fake.

The *second* one-minute post shooting drill is the power to the middle move. Instructions one through three for executing the power to the baseline move apply to the proper execution of this move. The defender, however, has taken away the baseline. After looking over her shoulder to the middle, she does not see a defender, so she takes a large step across the middle of the key with the foot closest to the free throw line, thus keeping the defender behind her. She dribbles once between her knees, squares to the basket, and shoots the shot.

The *third* one-minute shooting drill is the turnaround jumper. This shot is taken when the defensive player chooses to sag and play directly behind the post player, hoping to take away either the baseline or middle move. The player looks over her shoulder and sees the defender directly behind her. She pivots on her foot closest to the baseline and shoots a "bank" shot.

It should be noted that the backboard should be used on all three moves. It should also be added that a post player must use the dribble sparingly as the post area is very crowded and a dribble can easily be deflected. Only one dribble should be used, and it should be protected by putting it right between the knees.

If we had a choice, we would prefer to power to the baseline every time because it is the closest to the basket and therefore our highest percentage shot. Our philosophy of looking over our shoulder to the middle every time is refuted by many coaches, as they argue that you need to look where you would want to go first. We have selected to have our players look to the middle for the following reasons:

1. Looking to the middle often causes the defender to be faked into taking away the middle, thus leaving our favorite avenue to the basket open,

2. The middle is more crowded, so if we are forced to go there, we need to be looking at the situation at hand to make the appropriate decision.

To help our players make the right decision, as with the pump fake, later in the players' development, we position a defender inside the key below the free throw line. A player may position herself one of three ways. She may be crouched low with her hands down ready to steal, tie up, or deflect the dribble. If this is the case, the offensive player pulls the ball over this defender's head as she steps middle, and dribbles the ball closer to her lead foot. If the defensive player is playing tall with her hands above her waist, the offensive player fakes the crossover and dribbles one time quickly beneath the defender's hands as she steps across the key. Should the defensive player position herself to take away the middle and attempt to "sandwich" the post player between her and the baseline player, the offensive player fakes the power to the middle move by jab stepping up the key toward the free throw line, then pivots on her baseline foot, using a head and shoulder fake to give the baseline defender the impression of shooting a turnaround jumper. As the defender along the baseline raises up to pressure the shot, the offensive player uses a crossover move to step between the defenders and shoots a power layup.

An additional defender may be added to harass the passer. The passer holds the ball in triple threat position and passes it past the defender using one of the three passing zones:

1. right by the defender's ear,

2. right by the defender's hip, or

3. right over the top of the defender's head.

As you can see, the shooting form drills progress in the degree of difficulty depending upon the skill level of the players. The rotation of the initial drill was from player one to two to three to one on the other side of the basket. The rotation for the drill with the two additional defensive players (see Diagram 4-5) is from one to two to three to four to five and back to one on the other side. The post drills can be done in competition, as described in the first three one-minute shooting form drills.

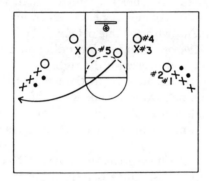

Diagram 4-5. Post Shooting Drill with Defenders on the Passer and Help in the Middle

Layup Drills

It is not unusual to see a coach explode when one of his/her players misses a layup during the course of a game. It is true that a layup is the easiest shot in basketball, but unless players practice layups on a daily basis, they are apt to miss them in a game situation. Aside from not allowing enough practice time for layups, other reasons for missing layups in game situations are as follows:

1. Incorrect shooting form,

2. Failure to protect the shot,

3. Going too fast, and

4. Feeling the pressure.

Therefore, the layup drills we use are designed and implemented into our program with these considerations in mind.

VARIATIONS OF THE LAYUP

Layups are a part of our pre-season workout schedules. During this time, we work not only on the correct shooting form for shooting the basic layup shot, but we teach variations of the layup.

The first variation to the basic layup is used when the offensive player sees some "daylight" between two defensive players. We practice this move by placing a chair on the square alongside of the key, and one inside the key about two feet from the other chair. Players line up on the hash marks on either side of the court, so both sides of the basket can be worked. The first player on the right side dribbles with her right hand directly toward the chair (make-believe defender) on the square. At the last second, she changes the ball to her left hand and steps through the two chairs sideways turning her back to the chair on the square. By turning her back to this defender, she has taken her out of the picture and has only to contend with the one defender she is now facing. She is to pull the ball over her or under her depending on her defensive stance. The shot is taken off both feet with the right foot forward on the right side, and shot with the left hand with the left foot forward on the left side. A jump stop can be used to step between the two defensive players. This, coupled with the action of the player going to the basket off of two feet (see Diagram 4-6) makes the move explosive, hence the name power layup.

To make this drill competitive, the players are challenged to make 40 baskets in two minutes. Should a player miss a shot during the course of the drill, she must quickly run a lap before rotating to the line on the other side of the basket. The players are instructed to get their own rebound and take the ball with them to the line they are rotating to, handing it to the next shooter in line. The drill starts off with two balls in each line, so that the players in the lines can take turns shooting at the basket without interruption. The players are also encouraged to use a jab fake before beginning the dribble toward the basket. If the players do not make 40 baskets in two minutes, they quickly do ten "heel touches" before starting the next layup drill.

The power slide variation to the basic layup shot has the same stipulations and formation as the power layup drill. The two chairs remain on the square on each side of the lane, but the chairs in the middle of the key are removed. This layup move is used by an offensive player driving the baseline, so the players dribble toward the baseline taking a giant step toward the basket once they have cleared their make-believe defender (see Diagram 4-7). The shot is once again taken by having the player explode to the basket off both feet. This, combined with the sliding action of the sideways giant step, gives it the name power slide.

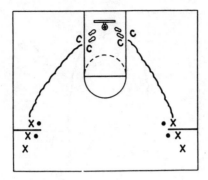

Diagram 4-6. Power Layup Drill

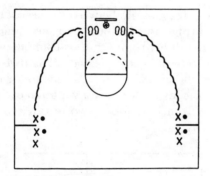

Diagram 4-7. Power Slide Drill

The layback is a variation that is used when the offensive player passes under the basket before releasing the shot. Our favorite drill to teach the layback has the same stipulations and formation, except that the players are lined up on hash marks that are extended and even with width of the key. The first player in the right line dribbles with her right hand down the side of the lane toward the chair (imaginary defender) on the right square of the lane. At the last instant, she uses a behind-the-back dribble to put the ball in her left hand. She continues the dribble across the key and under the basket shooting a left-handed layup on the left-hand side of the basket (see Diagram 4-8). The shot is released off of the right foot on the left side just as in the basic layup. Some coaches prefer using a semi-hook shot in this particular situation, but we ask our players to turn in midair and face the basket before releasing the shot.

The final variation to the layup that we teach is called the cross-over layup. The stipulations and formation for the drill is the same as that of the layback. The first player in line dribbles down the right side of the key directly toward the chair on the square. Upon reaching the

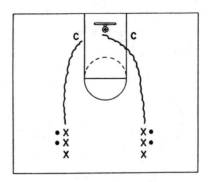

Diagram 4-8. Lay-Back Drill

chair, she plants her left foot right between the legs of the chair (imaginary defender) and brings the ball up over her head while stepping around the defender with her right leg, thus using the left foot as a pivot foot. The shot is a power layup released off both feet with the body turned sideways and the offensive player's back to the defender.

Our favorite basic layup drill is our variation of the Russian Layup Drill. Players rotate from line one to two to three to four and back to

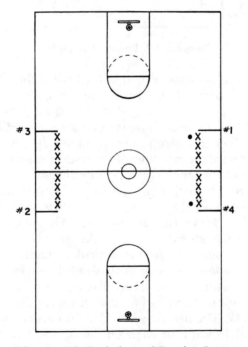

Diagram 4-9. Variations of Russian Layups

one, thus having to run the full length of the court before shooting or rebounding. We use this drill to emphasize correct form, and the importance of shooting under control in spite of fatigue. The first player in line one and line four have a ball. The player in line one shoots a right-handed layup and the one in line four a left-handed layup (see Diagram 4-9). Four minutes are put up on the clock. The players have to make 100 baskets before the buzzer sounds. On the right side, the ball must be shot with the right hand and off of the left foot, and on the left side, the ball must be shot with the left hand off of the right foot. To encourage hustling and good timing on the rebound, the ball cannot touch the floor. Should any of the above three stipulations not be met during the drill, the score goes back to the nearest decimal. For instance, if they have made 15 baskets and someone fails to shoot the ball with her left hand on the left side, the score goes back to 10. If the players fail to make 100 baskets at the end of four minutes, they have to run a horse.

The best pressure layup drill that I know of is referred to as pro-rolls. Using the two full courts in our gymnasium, we have the players divide into groups of three for a full-court figure eight drill (see Diagram 4-10). Only three passes and no dribbles are allowed per trip the full

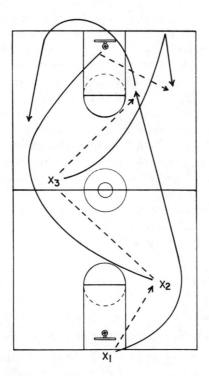

Diagram 4-10. "Pro-Rolls" Layup Drill

length of the court. In other words, player one passes to player two and runs behind her. Player two passes to player three and runs behind her. Player three passes the ball to player one who shoots the layup. Player two rebounds and passes the ball to player three who has touched the end line and is headed back to the other basket. The drill continues with the three passes and figure-eight action for one minute.

We like to use this drill at the end of our after-school practices. Each group of three has to make five layups within the one-minute time frame to be able to go to the dressing room. If they do not meet the requirement, they rest one minute and then go again. The three passes require the players to be going at full speed, thus the players learn to shoot under control regardless of their speed. They are also under pressure to make every layup as they rarely have time for more than one miss.

Free Throw Drills

Improper shooting form, lack of confidence, lack of concentration, and sheer panic are the reasons that most often cause players to miss critical free throws in game situations. For example, in the state tournament this year, I saw a Senior girl break out in tears knowing that there were two seconds left on the clock with her team one point behind, and she was going to the free throw line to shoot a one-and-one. (A player who had prepared herself would have looked upon this situation as the opportunity of a lifetime. She would have been practicing for this occasion during her entire junior high and high school career.) Although this girl was the leading scorer of her team, she was not emotionally prepared for this crisis. Needless to say, she missed the shot and will probably never forget that miss for the rest of her life.

Once a month throughout the entire school year, my students and I file out of the gym in an orderly fashion for a fire drill, making our way to the school parking lot where we wait for a signal that the drill is over. A ritual as to how we line up and how we exit the building has been established—and would probably keep us from total panic should the drill be for real. In all areas of life, it has been proven that a well-established ritual prevents panic in a crisis situation. For that reason, we have our players use the following ritual in shooting their free throws:

1. Approach the line and put the big toe of your right foot (if you are right-handed and left foot if you are left-handed) in a straight line with the middle of the basket. Your feet should be comfortably apart.

2. Bounce the ball (the same number of times each time).

3. Take a deep breath and let it out slowly as you *pinpoint* the rim.

4. Take a second to imagine that you are shooting a one-and-one.

You have just made the first one. How did it look? What trajectory (arch) did it take to go into the basket? Now take the shot.

5. Follow through until the ball goes through the basket.

6. Step off the line and repeat the same ritual.

During pre-season and post-season workouts, we have what is called a free throw challenge by correspondence with some neighboring schools. We have two teams of five players each. They each shoot 20 free throws per week. The results are mailed to one another. The losing teams have to send the winning teams a card, poster, etc., congratulating the winners. During this time, we video our players and carefully analyze their shooting form and ritual.

During our after-school workout sessions, we have two-minute free throw shooting sessions along with our water break. We have three players at a basket. Each player takes turns shooting two free throws. If a player makes both, she's allowed to get a drink quickly and then return to the drill. If she makes one of the two, she awaits her turn to shoot again. If she misses both, she must sprint to the other end of the gym and touch the wall, and then return to her assigned basket to await her turn to shoot again.

At the end of the workout, we put three minutes on the clock. Two players are assigned per basket. Each player will shoot a one-and-one. If she misses the first one, that's all she takes. If she makes the first one, she shoots once more.

After both players have shot, they kneel down on one knee. This stops the clock. The coach quickly points toward each basket, which signals the players to shout out the number of baskets made at their goal. If the team shot 100 percent, there would be the possibility of 24 baskets being made. As the players call out their scores, the coach quickly adds up the total. If 18 or more baskets are made (75 percent or better), the team gets to go in. If not, the clock is started and they shoot again. The procedure is repeated time after time until 75 percent accuracy is achieved or the three minutes have expired. If the challenge has not been met at the end of three minutes, the team has to do six minutes of pro-rolls, as described in the layup drill section of this chapter.

Jump Shot Drills

There is a myriad of jump shot drills a coach could use to increase the shooting proficiency of his/her players. The question that you must answer, however, is how much workout time should be spent on these drills. As regimented as our schedule is, outside of the shooting form drills, we do not have time for jump shot drills performed by the entire team. We do, however, have several favorite drills that are assigned to certain individuals of small groups who are not involved in a workout scrimmage. As was discussed in Chapter 1, unless you have only ten players on the team, some of your players will not be involved in scrimmage situations. You must make the decision as to the best method of utilizing their time. We frequently have them work on a competitive shooting drill, with a fellow player or manager keeping score.

One of the requirements of the guard position is the ability to shoot off of the dribble. A drill which we have our guards work on while waiting for their turn to scrimmage is simply called the "guard shooting drill." In this drill (see Diagram 4-11) a manager stands under the basket and signals to the player dribbling up whether she is to shoot from behind the middle cone (hand signal showing "stop"), the right cone (hand signal pointing right), or from the left cone (hand signal pointing left). The drill is timed on a stopwatch and the number of baskets made is recorded by the manager. The guard "taps" another guard out of the scrimmage, and she in turn performs the drill. After all of the guards have taken their turn, the poorest performer has to do ten fingertip push-ups.

According to our philosophy, we allow the wing players to take only two dribbles before having to pass or shoot. The shooting drill we use to develop our forwards' play is called the "forward shooting drill." The stipulations for the timing, scoring, and loser's punishment are the same as described in the guard shooting drill. However, the formation and technique are different (see Diagram 4-12).

As the manager passes the ball to the wing player, she takes a giant step toward the basket with the foot closest to the baseline. If the manager hollers "shot," she puts it up immediately from behind the middle cone. If she hollers "right," she puts the ball in triple threat position, jabs left, drives right using only two dribbles, and puts the ball up from behind the baseline cone. If she hollers "left," she assumes triple threat position, uses a head and shoulder fake to the right, drives left using only two dribbles, and puts the ball up from behind the left cone. It should be noted that from the right side, the giant step would be taken with the right foot, which becomes the pivot foot. Therefore the player cannot jab right. She could use a jab, lean, and go move with the left foot. (The jab, lean, and go technique will be explained later in this chapter under high post moves.) After one and one-half minutes, she moves to the left side of the floor to continue the three-minute drill.

Our post players do a drill which we call the "popout" shooting drill. Its stipulations for timing, scoring, and running are identical to the guard and forward shooting drills. The player posts up alongside of the key with a cone placed in front of her (see Diagram 4-13). She fakes one way and then "pops out" of the post to either cone. As the manager passes the ball to her, she takes a giant step toward the basket and puts the shot up on receiving the pass from behind the cone. After one and

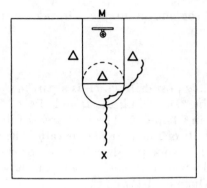

Diagram 4-11. Guard Shooting Drill

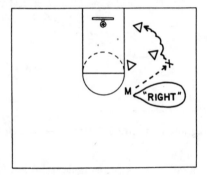

Diagram 4-12. Forward Shooting Drill

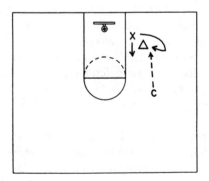

Diagram 4-13. Post Shooting Drill

one-half minutes, she moves to the left side of the court for the remainder of the drill.

Low Post Drills

Our favorite low post drill which is a part of our MWF defensive workout drills is the "Defending the Double Post." This drill will be described in detail in Chapter 5. The lead-up drill that we use to teach the fundamental skills of low post play is called the single post in the box drill. Using white shoe polish, which can be easily removed from the floor without damage to its surface, a box is drawn designating the low post area (see Diagram 4-14).

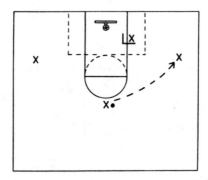

Diagram 4-14. Single Post in the Box Drill

An offensive player posts up alongside the key; a defensive player takes a cover-out stance. The drill begins with the ball at the point. The perimeter players are allowed to use only bounce passes in passing the ball into the post. They are also told not to hold the ball, but to pass it around to the other perimeter players, giving the post player a better opportunity to keep the post defender behind her. The defender is instructed to cover-out when the ball is on the point and to front when the ball is on the wing. The offensive player is free to move anywhere inside the box to try to position herself for a pass. Upon receiving the ball, she tries to score using one of the three low post moves described in the shooting form drills. If the defender gets the ball or if the shot is made, the ball is quickly passed back to the point player and the drill continues. After one minute, new offensive and defensive players enter the box.

The drill continues until all the players have taken their turn playing offense and defense. It should be noted that three-second lane violations will be called just as they would in a game. Each basket counts one point, with the losing team having to run a sprint at the end of the drill.

High Post Drills

There are three high post moves we teach during our high post shooting drills (see Diagram 4-15). The first is called the "jab, crossover, and dribble" move. Holding the ball in triple threat position, player number one jabs toward the basket with the leg closest to the sideline. Then she crosses over bringing it high over the defender's head and dribbles diagonally across the lane with her left hand for a left-handed layback. She gets her own rebound and takes the ball with her to line number two and gives the ball to the next player (X_5 or 0_5) in line.

Three balls should be used at each basket to assure fluid rotation. As soon as player number one starts her dribble to the basket, player number two starts her jab, crossover. She dribbles diagonally across the lane with her right hand for a right-handed layback. She gets her own rebound, takes the ball with her to line one and gives the ball to the next in line. Players continue to rotate from line one to two and vice-versa until the drill ends. Should a player improperly execute the high post move or miss the shot, she must quickly sprint to the other end of the gym and back without missing her turn.

At the end of two minutes, the clock buzzer sounds off signaling players to change to the "jab, rocker, shot" move. Once again, holding

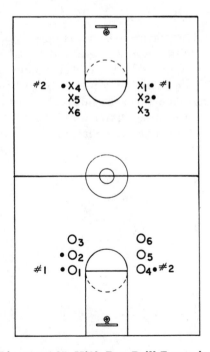

Diagram 4-15. High Post Drill Formations

the ball in triple threat position, player number one jabs toward the basket with the leg closest to the sideline. She then brings her feet back to shooting position and shoots a jump shot. The rebounding, rotation, and running stipulations remain the same.

The buzzer signals a change to the "jab, lean and go" move for the final two minutes of the drill. Once again, out of the triple threat position, player number one jabs as before. This time, however, she leans back at the waist, but keeps the foot, with which she jabbed, planted forward. The backward lean from the waist up gives this move the impression that the player has rocked back to shoot a jumper off the floor. As an imaginary defender raises up to pressure the shot, she drives down the right side of the key dribbling with her right hand, and shoots a right-handed layup. The rebounding, rotation, and running stipulations remain the same. It should be noted that only two dribbles are allowed in driving to the basket, and that the losing team will have to run at the end of this six-minute drill.

Our favorite high post drill is the one-on-one from the free throw line drill of our MWF defensive workout drills (see Chapter 5). These three high post moves are also used in properly executing the Hi-Lo Action, Pass Opposite, and Triple Post Rotation Drills of our TT offensive workout drills (see Chapter 12).

Under-the-Basket Drills

As with the missed layup, coaches simply come unglued when a player fails to score with a jumper right under the basket. Once again, although it is an easy shot, under-the-basket shooting must be practiced.

We often have the winning teams of a drill use this under-the-basket drill (see Diagram 4-16) at the side baskets, while the losing team is running on the main floor. Player number one shoots a jump shot and runs to the end of the other line. Player number two jumps up to get

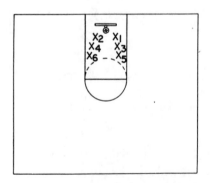

Diagram 4-16. Under-the-Basket Shooting Drill

the rebound and shoots it back up and runs to the other end of the line. Player number three must now jump up to rebound and put it up, etc. The drill continues for one minute.

To make sure the drill is challenging, the players can be instructed that they must make 15 baskets by the end of the drill. If the ball should hit the floor, the count goes back to the nearest decimal—0 or 10. Should they not meet the challenge, they have to run.

Shooting drills are fun and productive, and the possibility for formations are endless. However, coaches must be selective in designing drills which will not only increase shooting proficiency, but will be beneficial to their philosophy and suitable to the time slot allotted for shooting drills in their workout schedule.

5

Using Competitive Drills To Teach One-On-One Offensive And Defensive Plays

Having ascertained that our program is indeed defensive-oriented, let us take a closer look at our Monday-Wednesday-Friday defensive drills.

It is our philosophy that there are four basic fundamental defensive stances which must be mastered by our players to have a successful pressure man-for-man defensive team. They are as follows:

1. Hawking the ball—that is, putting pressure on a dribbler outside of the scoring area,

2. Defending a player who has just received the ball in the scoring area and who has her dribble left,

3. Denying the pass to the perimeter players—that is, off-the-ball defense of the forward and guard positions, and

4. Denying the pass to the post area.

As stated before, we teach the stances in mass drill and then practice their execcution in four MWF drills.

PRESSURING THE DRIBBLER

The purpose of this one-on-one full court drill is to teach a defensive player how to put pressure on a dribbler outside of the scoring area. The name of this drill is "Hawking the Ball" as this is the terminology we use to refer to pressuring the dribbler.

Hawking the Ball Drill

For the Hawking the Ball drill, chairs are placed down the length of the court from free throw line to free throw line, to divide the court into two equal halves (see Diagram 5-1). The squad is divided into two teams—a red team and a blue team. On one half of the floor, the player is on offense; on the other, she will play defense. Five minutes are put up on the clock. The players are instructed that if a player scores on them or if they fail to score during the drill, they must run a bleacher before taking their place in line. Should they miss their turn at any time during the drill by taking too much time in running the bleacher, their entire team, red or blue, will have to run a horse at the end of the drill.

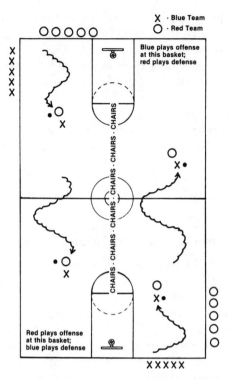

Diagram 5-1. One-on-One Full Court

At the end of five minutes, the losing team will have to run a horse while the winning team does a shooting drill on the side baskets. One point is awarded per basket. Points are tallied on the scoreboard. On the coach's whistle, the players begin playing one-on-one the full length of the court. The offensive players are not allowed to use a reverse dribble.

The Correct Defensive Stance

The defensive players are, of course, motivated to use the correct defensive stance, as the coach's evaluation of their performance in the drill will determine whether or not they will be issued their basketball leggings or game hose. The stipulation that players will have to run for failing to score or allowing a score, plus the team having to run for losing or for a lack of hustle in running the bleachers by a teammate, are added incentives.

In all of our defensive stances, we want our players to make themselves as big as possible in order to take up as much floor space as possible. In guarding the dribbler, players are to get their feet wide apart with their toes and knees pointing slightly outward. They bend their knees, keeping their hips down, and assume, what is called, a heel-toe stance. This means that the toes of their back foot are in a line even with the heel of their front foot.

If the person a player is guarding is dribbling with her right hand, the defensive player keeps her right foot forward. If she is dribbling with her left hand, the defender keeps her left foot forward. It is important that the defensive players keep their hips parallel to take up as much floor space as possible. If a player gets out of her heel-toe stance and turns sideways to the dribbler, we call it *opening the gate*. The area occupied by the defensive player becomes very narrow, and the dribbler can drive right past her. The defensive player must always remember that she wants to keep the middle of her chest in the direction the dribbler is moving.

The Basic Rule in Guarding the Dribbler

The basic rule in guarding the dribbler is that the defender must keep her body between the person she is guarding and the basket. She does this by shuffling her feet in such a manner so that the back foot does all of the work by retreating at a 45-degree angle quickly, but only 6 to 12 inches at a time. The front foot stays in contact with the floor, so that a change in direction by the dribbler may be countered more quickly by what we call a *drop-step* action. The heel-toe stance is maintained, but the opposite foot is now forward.

We advocate a sliding action, rather than a churning action, of the feet to facilitate quicker reaction to a change of direction. The feet must push off of the floor in order to change the heel-toe stance from right foot forward to left foot forward should the offensive player change from dribbling to her right and head to the left. If the player is using a churning action, the split-second that her foot is not in contact with the floor, making it impossible to push off the floor at that instant, may provide the offensive player with adequate time to drive past the defensive player. The feet stay wide apart. Should a player allow her feet to come together, she covers only a small area of the floor making her susceptible to the drive.

How the Hands Can Put Additional Pressure on the Dribbler

Defense is, of course, played primarily with the feet, but the hands can put a lot of pressure on the person being guarded if the defensive players can follow a few simple rules.

First of all, we want the players' arms straight and extended in front of them. The palms of the hands face the ball, with the fingers pointed upward ready to "shadow" the ball. This means the hands will remain in the same plane as the ball. Second, we want the defenders to shake their hands frantically, wildly, as close to the ball as possible without losing their balance or reaching. Last, their elbows must always stay inside the vertical line of their knees. If their arm goes outside this vertical line, this indicates that they are reaching and that they have quit moving their feet. This not only allows the person they are guarding to move past them, but should the offensive player make contact with her extended arms, the defender will be charged with a foul.

The Most Common Errors of Execution

Now that the proper defensive stance for pressuring the dribbler has been established (see Photo 1), let us take a look at a checklist of the most common errors of execution (according to our philosophy) that

Photo 1

players encounter while performing the one-on-one full court hawking the ball drill. This checklist is used to evaluate individual performances. It should be noted that the checklist is coded to facilitate in the evaluations of the videotaped practice sessions. As discussed in Chapter 1, the evaluations are recorded on our mass drill charts so that players may readily interpret their critiques and recognize those points of execution that must be improved before they can "earn their uniform"— their game hose, in this particular drill.

ONE-ON-ONE FULL COURT

Code	Improper Execution
KB	KNEES NOT BENT
FT	FEET COMING TOGETHER
OG	OPENING GATE
SS	SHUFFLE TOO SLOWLY
45	FAILURE TO SHUFFLE AT 45-DEGREE ANGLE
RU	RUNNING TOO MUCH
L	PLAYING TOO LOOSE
H	IMPROPER MOVEMENT OF HANDS
EL	ELBOWS OUTSIDE OF KNEES
R	REACHING
D	FAILURE TO HOLLER "DEAD" (WHEN THE DRIBBLER PICKS UP THE BALL ALERTING TEAMMATES TO DENY EVERY PASS "TOUGH" AND PERHAPS GAIN POSSESSION OF THE BALL ON A 5-SECOND VIOLATION)
BU	FAILURE TO BELLY UP ONCE THE PLAYER GETS INSIDE THE SCORING AREA
BO	FAILURE TO BLOCK OUT
BT	FAILURE TO KEEP BUTT DOWN

To make sure that everyone understands the underlying philosophy governing the rules of execution for this particular drill, we give our players a written or oral test over the following simply stated points of our philosophy.

PRESSURING THE DRIBBLER

1. *You are not trying to steal the ball off the dribbler.* When she gets tired enough, she will hand it to you. You

must first harass her to the point of exhaustion, and then be ready to capitalize on it!

2. Place legs wide apart. Knees and toes pointed outward slightly. *Butt down.*

3. Try to harass the playmaker—not steal the ball. Therefore, your first responsibility is: *Keep Her From Penetrating.* Shake your hands to make her nervous, but above all, *STOP THE DRIVE!*

4. Do not reach. It will merely cause you to lose your balance and to stop moving your feet. Your man will drive by you.

5. *Scream when they pick up the ball.*

6. *Wave Your Hands Frantically.*

7. All of you *Must Shuffle.* Take pride in your defense. Everyone else runs, but Victoria *SHUFFLES*—that is why we are Number One!

Offensive Play Instructions

With all of this concentration on defensive execution, the offensive play instructions are kept to a minimum. The players are told to work on their various dribbling techniques such as exchange, double exchange, stutter, backward and behind the back. Reverse dribbles are not allowed, as we do not want our offensive personnel not facing the basket while dribbling outside the scoring area. We feel that the reverse dribble is most susceptible to steals, traps, and charging fouls against a good defensive team.

Players are expected to follow the basic rules of dribbling. The dribbler should bend her knees and bend at the waist assuming a crouched position. The ball should be dribbled close to the hip to keep her body between the ball and the defender. There will be a slight pumping action of the arm and upper shoulder, but the direction of the ball is controlled by the fingertips. The dribbler should keep her head up. We tell our players not to look at the ball as there is nothing to see. The ball hits the floor and comes right back to their hand. They can see this action out of the corner of their eye, so there is no need to put their head down.

Players must learn to look up while dribbling in order to be able to see what is going on. To emphasize this, we occasionally station a manager behind each basket. They signal in various ways, such as touching the top of their heads, waving, showing a closed fist, etc. The offensive dribbler must mimic with her free hand what the manager has signaled. If she fails to mimic the manager's signal, she has to run a sprint for each failure after practice. Using the mass drill chart (see Chapter 1), the managers tally each failure.

"ON THE BALL" DEFENSE IN THE SCORING AREA

The heel-toe stance is most effective when guarding the dribbler outside the scoring area, as it allows the defensive player the proper angles to send the dribbler to the sideline. Should the defender be backed into the key, she assumes a parallel stance putting both hands up to possibly deflect a shot. The defender must remember to keep moving her feet. If the offensive player stops dribbling in the scoring area, the defender "belly's up" to her. This means getting as close to the offensive player as possible without touching, so that the defender can crowd the player and possibly cause her to fall back on the shot.

The arms are extended straight up with the fingers of the hands spread apart ready to "shadow" the ball, or to try to put a hand on the ball should she attempt to shoot. She should also holler "DEAD! DEAD! DEAD!" to alert teammates the ball has been picked up and they need to deny the pass to their offensive player to create a five-second count violation or a three-second violation should the ball be in the key. When the ball goes up, the defender needs to holler "Shot" to alert teammates to block out.

The Stance a Player Should Assume

The stance a player assumes to guard a player who has just received the ball in the scoring area is a slight variation to the stance described to guard a dribbler. As the defensive player approaches the player with the ball, she puts one hand over the ball. This keeps the player from being able to bring the ball up to shoot. She will now have to pass, dribble, or jab fake, so the defensive player must have her knees bent with good balance and be ready to move. Her other hand is extended in back and to the side of her with her fingers spread wide apart to possibly deflect a pass, but more importantly, to feel for the possibility of anyone setting a screen (see Photo 2).

One-on-One from the Free Throw Line

Our favorite drill to teach this aspect of defensive play is named "One-on-one from the Free Throw Line." Its purpose is to teach players how to defend a player who is in the scoring area with the ball and has

Photo 2

the dribble left. This drill will once again be done in competition with the same stipulations for running, as described for the Hawking the Ball drill. The same scoring system will also be used for this five-minute drill. Teams will play defense on one end of the court and offense on the other.

The drill begins by having the defensive player standing under the basket and rolling the ball toward the offensive player standing at the top of the circle (see Diagram 5-2). The offensive player rushes forward to pick up the ball at the free throw line. The players will play one-on-one, with the offensive player limited to two dribbles to encourage her to use good fakes and direct movement to the basket. Evaluations of players' performance in this drill will determine whether or not they will be issued their game shorts.

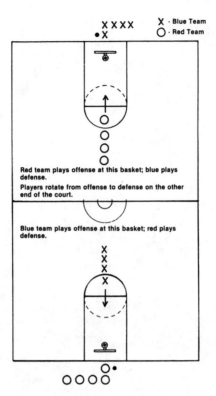

Diagram 5-2. One-on-One from the Free Throw Line

A checklist of the most common errors of execution according to our philosophy that players encounter while performing the "One-on-one from the Free Throw line" drill is as follows:

ONE-ON-ONE FROM THE FREE THROW LINE

Code	Improper Execution
R	REACHING
OB	FAILURE TO PUT HAND OVER THE BALL
HB	FAILURE TO HAVE OTHER HAND BACK FOR SCREEN
S	FAILURE TO SHUFFLE CORRECTLY
TS	TURNING SIDEWAYS TO THE DRIBBLER
BU	FAILURE TO BELLY UP

FM   FAILURE TO KEEP FEET MOVING WHILE BELLIED
        UP

H   FAILURE TO PUT HANDS UP ON THE SHOT

J   JUMPING TOO MUCH ON THE FAKE

BO   FAILURE TO BLOCK OUT TOUGH

To make sure that everyone understands the underlying philosophy governing the rules of execution for this particular drill, we give our players a written or oral test over the following rules of our philosophy:

ONE-ON-ONE PLAY WHEN THE BALL IS IN THE SCORING AREA WITH THE DRIBBLE LEFT

You are not trying to steal the ball if your man catches it in the scoring area. You are stopping the shot first, so HAND OVER THE BALL. Be ready to shuffle. Be ready to belly up—not sideways, but facing the player.

The rules of execution for a one-on-one play are:

Offensive Player's Checklist

1. Hold ball in triple threat position.

2. Face the basket.

3. Be *aware* of the basket at all times.

4. Your goal should be to get as close to the basket as possible before you shoot.

5. Always fake at least once.

6. Give your defender time to react to the fake.

7. Always use your left hand when going left and your right hand when going right.

8. Keep your body between your defender and the ball.

Defensive Player's Checklist

1. Run to meet your opponent, but go under control.

2. Take a good defensive stance—feet wide apart, usually a parallel stance; knees bent, rear-end down, balanced and

ready to move (shuffle) in either direction. Usually play "straight"—your head is in line with the head of the offensive player.

3. Play hand over the ball. Other hand feeling.

4. Keep feet wide apart during the shuffle. Do not bob up and down. Stay low.

5. When the player gets ready to shoot (in fact, when she gets in the lower part of the key or within that range from the side), "belly up"! Get both hands up and crowd the offensive player. Do not lean on her, but be within one inch of her. Keep your feet moving until the offensive player stops. Holler at her to distract her.

6. When the player prepares to shoot, don't leave the floor until her feet leave.

7. Try to put your hand on the ball, not necessarily to block the shot.

A tall offensive player on a short defender should score every time. When they are the same size, the offensive player should be able to score every time. Therefore, evenly matched or shorter players need to keep their girl from dribbling into the scoring area, and they must never allow their girl to receive the ball in the scoring area.

"OFF THE BALL" DEFENSE IN THE SCORING AREA

The stance the defender assumes to guard a player without the ball will vary with the location of that player on the court. If the player the defender is guarding is one pass away from the ball, the defensive player assumes what we call a tight cover-out stance (see Photo 3).

First, the defender puts her body between her man and the basket. Then she puts one leg and one arm between her man and the ball. She must look over her shoulder so that she can see her man and the ball simultaneously using her peripheral vision. The palm of her hand should be opened toward the ball. This is important in case she deflects the ball, so that she can control it or push it in the direction she wants it to go. If the offensive player moves back, the defensive player shuffles backward to stay with her; if the player moves forward, she shuffles with her. If the player breaks behind her, the defensive player opens up toward the ball so that she is ready to go for an interception if a pass is attempted to be thrown over the defender's head (see Photo 4). If the offensive player she is guarding moves to the other side of the basket, the

Photo 3

defensive player assumes her cover-out stance again, except she denies the pass with the opposite leg and arm.

Our favorite drill designed to teach off-the-ball defense of the perimeter players is called the "Tiger" or Cover-Out Drill. The same stipulations for running and scoring, as described in the two defensive drills already introduced, will be employed in this five-minute drill, except that players will run and touch the opposite gym wall instead of running a bleacher for individual failures. Offensive players without the ball take their position along the baseline (see Diagram 5-3). Her teammate, with the ball in the area of the free throw line extended, will attempt to pass the ball to the baseline player on the coach's verbal command of "GO." The coach begins an audible count of "one thou-

Photo 4

sand one, one thousand two, etc." If the baseline player has not received the ball due to the pass denial play of the defensive player by the time the coach has counted off five seconds, the baseline player must sprint to the opposite end of the gym before rotating to the next line assignment. Should the baseline player receive the ball within the five-second count, the two players play one-on-one following the same rules described in the one-on-one from the free throw line drill.

It should be noted that the offensive player is not allowed to move toward the passer any higher than the dotted line shown in the diagram. Since we want our offensive players to keep the offense as spread out as

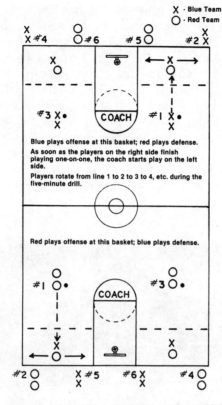

Diagram 5-3. "Tiger" or Cover-Out Drill

possible, they must learn to receive the ball in a restricted area. Unless the denial stance is extremely poor and a "backdoor" is easy picking, our wing players make their first move away from the ball in hope of setting up the defensive player for the "backdoor" option.

The wing players must be willing to work their tails off in receiving the ball, using the entire width of the court. When a wing player is playing along the baseline, she will make her initial move to within three feet of the sideline and then will try to hit the "backdoor." If this fails, she will "pop out" toward the sideline again. If the defender is exceptionally good, the player must execute a crossover move to receive the pass.

In the crossover move, the offensive player, while faking a second backdoor attempt, will suddenly plant the foot nearest the passer to use as a pivot foot. With the leg nearest the baseline, she will crossover or step around the defender toward the ball, extending the arm closest to the defender, straight toward the ball to deter the defender from being able to deflect the pass (see Photo 5). The arm farthest from the defender is extended out to the side giving a target for the pass away from the defender. If the denial is still adequate to deflect the pass, she takes two sliding steps toward the baseline giving the passer the opportunity to lead her with the pass, thus creating the farthest distance possible between the flight of the ball and the defender's outstretched arm. Upon receiving the ball, the player pivots to face the basket using a crossover move if she is crowded by the defense. She then puts the ball in triple threat position and follows the rules for one-on-one offensive play from the free throw line.

Photo 5

The most common errors of defensive play in this particular drill are as follows:

"TIGER" DRILL

Code	Improper Execution
KB	KNEES NOT BENT
P	PALM TO THE BALL
LS	NOT LOOKING OVER THE SHOULDER
TB	ALLOWING PLAYER TO MOVE TOWARD THE BALL
S	FAILURE TO SHUFFLE
L	FAILURE TO STAY LOW
NT	NOT TOUGH ENOUGH—HAVE TO SCRATCH
OU	FAILURE TO OPEN UP
H	HOOKING MAN WITH ARM
B	FAILURE TO CUT OFF BASELINE DRIVE
BD	FAILURE TO PROTECT THE BACKDOOR
SO	FAILURE TO SPREAD OUT WIDE IN STANCE
BU	FAILURE TO BELLY UP
BO	FAILURE TO BLOCK OUT
D	FAILURE TO ASSUME A GOOD DEFENSIVE STANCE ONCE PLAYER HAS RECEIVED THE BALL
J	JUMPING TOO MUCH

Once again, we give our players a written or oral test over a very simply stated philosophy governing the rules of execution for this particular drill. It is as follows:

"OFF THE BALL" DEFENSE OF
THE PERIMETER PLAYERS

You are not trying to steal the ball in your denial or cover-out stance. You are merely trying to keep your girl from catching the ball for a FIVE-SECOND COUNT. Do not lunge for the ball. Shuffle and maintain your stance. If she does receive the ball, make sure you put your *hand over the ball immediately.*

Post Play

If the player you are guarding is one pass away and in the post area, a combination of covering out and fronting will be used. When the ball is on the point, the defender will assume a cover-out stance. If the ball moves to the wing, the defender will front the post player ready to go for an interception if a pass is attempted to be thrown over the defender's head. If the ball moves to the corner, the post defender will front providing the offense is in a double low post set, so that backside help is available. Should the offense be in a high, low, or single post set, the post defender will cover out from the baseline side to influence the pass toward the middle where more help is available.

If the defensive player is guarding a player two passes away from the ball, she will use an open-up stance. With her back to the basket, her knees bent comfortably for quick mobility and good balance, she plays between her man and the ball. The farther her man is from the ball, the closer she plays toward the ball. She points one extended arm toward her player and another extended arm toward the ball. She looks straight ahead so that she can see the ball and also see her man using her peripheral vision. From this stance (see Photo 6), she can help out a fellow defender, yet quickly cover out on her player should she attempt to move toward the ball to receive the pass.

Our favorite drill to teach denying passes into the post area and also how to give backside help is called the "Defending the Double Post" drill. The offense sets up in a double low post set (see Diagram 5-4). The three outside players are not allowed to shoot the ball; they are allowed only to pass the ball around the periphery or into the post players.

Once again, this drill is done in competition with the scoring (the same as described in the other defensive drills). Two defensive players are assigned to guard the offensive players in the post area. The offensive players try to receive the pass from the outside players by posting up in their assigned areas. The defensive players employ denial, fronting, and rotation techniques to keep the ball from coming in to the post players. Should the ball be received into the post area, the defense must try to keep the post player from scoring. The drill lasts for one minute; then a new group of players are assigned into the post area with new defenders. The drill continues until all of the players have played both offense and defense at the post positions.

Photo 6

Rotation Rules

Our rules for giving backside help during this drill include the concept of rotation or changing defensive assignments. Our rules for rotation in this drill are as follows:

1. If a pass is attempted to your post player, you have the option of first going for the interception, but once the ball goes past you, you quickly roll off your player and go guard the other post player—or position yourself inside this post player for the rebound.

2. If you are the player giving backside help, your first option is to:
   A. go for the interception
   B. try to draw the charge
   C. take away the baseline, making the post player turn toward the middle where it is more crowded to take the shot.

The most common errors in the execution of this drill are as follows:

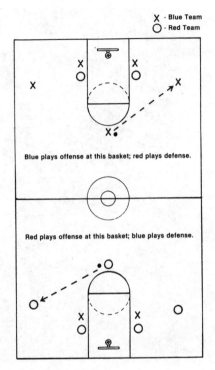

Diagram 5-4. Defending the Double Post Drill

DEFENDING THE DOUBLE POST

Code	Improper Execution
CO	FAILURE TO COVER-OUT WHEN THE BALL IS ON THE POINT
HAA	HAND AND ARM NOT HIGH ENOUGH ON COVER-OUT
BO	FAILURE TO BLOCK OUT
M	ALLOWING PLAYER TO CUT TO THE MIDDLE
H	HOOKING PLAYER WITH ARM
R	REACHING OVER PLAYER'S BACK TO DEFLECT THE BALL
F	FAILURE TO HOOK OFFENSIVE PLAYER WITH FOOT TO STAY IN FRONT
BET	FAILURE TO PLAY BETWEEN WHEN OPENED UP

BUP	FAILURE TO PLAY BETWEEN UNTIL THE BALL IS PASSED
BS	FAILURE TO GIVE BACKSIDE HELP IN TIME
I	FAILURE TO GO FOR THE INTERCEPTION
CH	FAILURE TO TAKE THE CHARGE
TM	FAILURE TO TURN THE PLAYER TO THE MIDDLE
ROT	FAILURE TO ROTATE QUICKLY
FO	FOULING WHEN GOING FOR THE INTERCEPTION

The offensive players should use the techniques for post play that were described in Chapter 4. Early in the season, the post players are restricted to the low post area on their respective sides of the basket. Further into the season, they are allowed to flash from the weakside low post area to the weakside high post area and later to the strongside high post area. Eventually the post players are allowed to cross, stack, or screen for one another. In other words, they are given a free reign in maneuvering to get the ball. The restrictions are removed gradually as the confidence of the defensive play is improved.

An oral or written test is given over this simply stated philosophy governing the rules of execution for this particular drill.

"OFF THE BALL" DEFENSE OF THE POST PLAYERS

The only time you are trying to steal the ball is when it is going into the post area. On the rotation:

1. You are trying to steal the pass. Come quickly and use good judgment.

2. You are trying to draw the *charge.*

3. You are not going to let them square to the basket to shoot the ball without having to reverse from their initial direction.

"GET TOUGH" DRILLS

Spring training is usually the time we concentrate on drills that will get our players used to physical contact with one another and hitting the floor. Although basketball is professed to be a non-contact sport, the championship level of basketball requires a great deal of physical contact. Our three favorite "get tough" drills are as follows:

Mat Basketball

This drill may be done two different ways, depending upon how much contact you want to expose your players to. If, for example, we have an especially timid group, we put several gym mats together on the floor and place a large plastic trash can on each end of the mat. Two players of similar size and strength get in the middle of the mats on their knees for a tip-off (similar to a jump ball). A manager or coach throws the ball up between them, and then anything—except for hitting, kicking, scratching, pinching, and hair pulling—goes. The object is for a player to gain possession of the basketball and slam dunk it in her assigned trash can. She can roll, crawl, etc., but cannot get up on her feet.

The defensive player can wrestle or tackle the player with the ball to keep her from scoring. In addition, she must try to gain possession of the ball by ripping it out of the opponent's grasp. If there is a tie ball that lasts ten seconds or longer, the players return to the middle of the mats for another tip-off. When a player succeeds in slamming the ball into a trash can, she is awarded two points, and another tip-off at "mid-mat" starts the action all over again. The drill can vary in length, but the players are usually on the mat for only two minutes at a time. At the end of the drill, the loser has to run a suicide (see Chapter 3).

A less physical version of the drill has the group divided into two teams. Two gym mats 12 feet long are placed side by side. The players line up one behind the other at the end of their respective mat. A mark, nine feet from the end of the mat where the players are lined up, is placed on each mat to indicate where a basketball will be placed. At the end of each mat, opposite the players, are placed two large plastic trash cans. The coach gives the commands "On your mark! Get set! Go!" On the word "Go!" the first player in each line dives for the basketball on her mat and quickly slam dunks it into her trash can. The slam to hit the bottom of the trash can first is awarded a point. The game is played for five minutes with the losing team having to run at the end of the drill.

German Football

Two teams of five or six are lined up along opposite sidelines facing one another. The players of each team are given a number of one through six. A towel is put in the middle of the free throw line, and two lines six feet apart indicating each team's goal are marked in the middle of each sideline. The coach calls out a number, and the player from each team who has that number runs out to retrieve the towel. Using only their feet, they try to slide it or kick it across the sideline inside their goal area. They can use their bodies to bump and push each other off the towel. To avoid elbowing, we have the players cross their arms so they can hold each elbow with their opposite hand, thus covering the bony and dangerous protusion of the elbows.

Each pair of players has 20 seconds to score. If one of them has not succeeded in scoring by then, they return to the sideline and the towel is once again placed on the free throw line awaiting the next "foot tug-of-war" between a pair of players whose number has been called. One point is awarded for each successful goal. We either play for five minutes, or the team scoring 15 points first wins. Individuals not scoring during the drill have to run a bleacher following their turn. At the end of the drill, the losing team has to run.

Loose Ball Drill

The coach stands in the mid-court circle holding a basketball. Two teams of players lined up one behind the other are restrained by the mid-court line. The coach may either roll the ball, bounce it straight up in the air, or throw it high into the air. As soon as it leaves the coach's hand, the first player in each line runs out to gain possession of the ball. Whoever gets the ball plays offense and tries to score a basket. The other player plays defense. The player scoring the basket is awarded one point. The player who failed to score has to run a sprint to the opposite end of the court.

The drill is five minutes long, with the losing team having to run at the end. There is a lot of contact in this drill as players dive after rolling balls. If the coach will take the ball above his/her head and bounce it against the floor as high as possible, the two players will crash against each other in midair. If the ball is thrown high into the air toward the basket, there will be a lot of contact while players are slapping at the ball to gain control.

After using these one-on-one get tough drills, you will find your players not hesitating to hit the floor or to make contact with another player after a loose ball. In fact, if you use all the drills described in this chapter on a regular basis, you will observe marked improvement in the aggressiveness and competitiveness of your team.

6 Teaching Players How to Capitalize on Mismatch Situations

In the game of basketball, as in most team sports, the most productive scoring opportunities arise from what I call mismatch situations. A potent offensive team is usually a team that is capable of creating such a situation in one of the following ways:

1. fast break,

2. penetration,

3. height advantage, or

4. an outstanding individual scorer.

An effective fast-breaking team tries to beat their opponents down the floor. This does not mean they hope to "outrun" all five of the opposing players, but they do hope to come down the floor quickly enough to momentarily outnumber the defensive players and, thus, increase their chance of scoring by skillfully taking advantage of a 2-on-1, 3-on-2, etc., situation.

Penetration, causing two defensive players to have to guard one offensive player, also creates a brief mismatch in numbers. For only an instant following effective penetration, four players have to defend five. For this reason, penetrating skills are often the key to a consistent scoring attack.

Gaining a height advantage is one of the most popular methods of capitalizing on a mismatch situation. Some teams simply have the good fortune of having a "giant" on their team; others slip tall perimeter players guarded by short defenders into the post; still others use screening and crossing tactics to force short defenders to have to guard tall offensive players.

An outstanding individual scorer who simply cannot be contained by conventional man-for-man or zone defenses frequently causes opposing teams to resort to a specialty-type of defense. The most popular specialty defensive sets are the box and 1, the diamond and 1, and the triangle and two. These man-zone combinations are extremely vulnerable to mismatch situations created by offensive overloading and screening tactics.

FAST BREAK SITUATIONS

Two-on-One Drills

A two-on-one situation is usually the end result of a fast break. Therefore, execution must be quick, simple, and very disciplined. Our players are given a checklist for proper execution of this particular skill (see Chapter 1). In summarizing the points of execution, it should be noted that it is the responsibility of the player without the ball to move to the side of the basket opposite the approaching dribbler. Players are allowed only one pass because, as we always tell our players, unless the opposing team have all been struck by lightning in the backcourt, they will all be charging down the floor to the aid of the sole defender. We also require that this pass be a bounce pass, because if the dribbler truly makes the sole defender commit herself to stopping the shot off the drive, the defender will almost always have her hands up. And too many passes are deflected and even intercepted by defenders with good timing and anticipation if the dribbler tries to pass over them.

Defensively, a player's first responsibility is to stop the drive. She should not go any higher than the free throw line in executing a series of defensive fakes, hoping to make the dribbler pick up the ball as far away from the basket as possible. This may give the defender time to drop back on the girl positioned under the basket, and it also may provide enough time for other defensive players to help out.

Our favorite half-court 2-on-1 drill is called "2-on-1 with a chaser." For this drill, five minutes are put on the clock. The red team is on offense first. The ball begins on the right side of the court at the mid-court line near the center circle. The other offensive line is positioned on the right side of the basket near the key. One defensive line is positioned under the basket. The first player in this line assumes a cover-out stance on the offensive player near the basket. Another defensive line is positioned behind the mid-court line extended on the right side of the court (see Diagram 6-1). This line is referred to as the "chaser" line.

When the coach blows the whistle, X_1 dribbles toward X_2 who clears toward the opposite side of the basket, positioning herself along the left side of the key with her left foot on the block. She is facing the dribbler either ready to receive the pass or to position herself for a rebound should X_1 shoot the ball. O_1 starts a series of defensive fakes as she sees the open player dribbling toward the key unguarded. O_2 runs toward the key hoping to stop the pass to X_2, or she may chase the dribbler trying to deflect the ball. She then goes along the baseline to try to stop the pass to X_2.

The chaser makes the offense execute quickly, but it also helps X_2 make the right decision as to how to receive and shoot the ball. If the chaser chooses to come across the key to stop the pass (see Diagram 6-2),

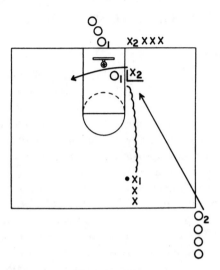

Diagram 6-1

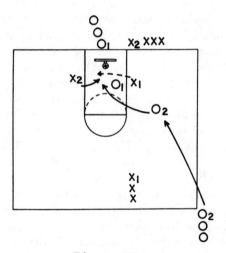

Diagram 6-2

X_2 steps toward the ball with her right foot to receive the pass. Upon receiving the pass, she pivots on her left foot which is located on the block alongside the key and turns her back to the free throw line, thus keeping her defender behind her. She shoots a jump shot off the board, keeping the ball well in front of her to avoid getting the shot blocked from behind. If the chaser chooses to try to deflect the ball off the dribble and is quick enough to try to stop the pass from the baseline side (see Diagram 6-3), the offensive player steps toward the pass with the foot closest to the baseline. Upon receiving the pass, she may shoot a right-

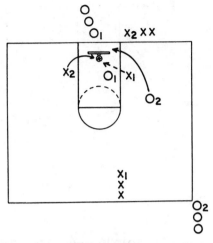

Diagram 6-3

handed lay-back straight between the two defenders, or she may fake the lay-back and shoot a turn-around jumper using the right foot as the pivot foot.

After one minute and fifteen seconds, the lines move to the left side of the court so that execution may be practiced from both sides. After two and one-half minutes, the teams change from offense to defense. The managers keep score by awarding one point for each basket that is made.

At the end of the drill, the losing team will have to run one suicide (see Chapter 3), while the winners do the under-the-basket drill on the side court (see Chapter 4). During the course of the drill, the players have to run if they do not score when on offense. This running usually consists of a lap or a sprint to the other end of the court. Another stipulation we often add is that the score will go to zero if the dribbler does not make the defensive player commit herself to stopping the drive before she passes, or if the player receiving the ball does not step toward the ball properly to protect it.

Three-on-Two Drills

We start off teaching proper execution of a 3-on-2 situation by first identifying the three lanes of the court—right, middle, and left. The first player in the middle line of each team begins the drill by passing to her teammate on either side of her. The receiving player in the side lane, whether it be the right lane or left lane, returns the pass back to the middle player. She now passes the ball to the player on the other side. This player returns the pass to the middle (see Diagram 6-4). This completes four passes, which means that the players should be in the area of

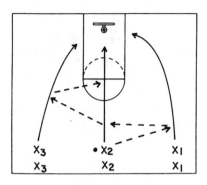

Diagram 6-4

the free throw line. When there is no score on the scoreboard clock at the end of the drill, it signals the player in the middle line to shoot a layup after four passes have been completed.

The managers keep score for each team, tallying one point per basket. If the score ends in an odd number such as one, three, fifteen, etc., this signals a layup from the left lane, so the middle man has to be alert to pass it back to the left side after four passes have been completed. If the score ends in an even number, this signals a layup from the right side, but only after four passes have been completed. Should the ball be shot from the wrong lane, the team's score goes back to the nearest decimal. The losing team has to run at the end of the drill.

To emphasize the importance of having the players stay in a triangle on a 3-on-2 situation, so that they cannot be easily guarded, we add two defenders to the straight-line break described above (see Diagram 6-5). The players can only score by shooting a layup. To keep the defense from anticipating where the layup is coming from, we give each team their own set of signals. In other words, a zero for the blue team may now signal a layup from the left side and a layup from the right side for the red team; or any other combination or system of signaling that each team decides on.

In the unguarded straight-line drill, the players rotated from line one to two to three and back to one. They now rotate to the defensive lines four and five before going back to one. The losers once again have to run at the end of the drill.

This guarded straight-line drill is good offensively as it teaches players how to fake the pass and shoot the layup. Defensively, it is an excellent drill for teaching players how to take the charge. In fact, a team committing a charging foul has their score go back to zero as added incentive to take the charge. Our main purpose for using this drill, however, is to make it quite apparent that two defenders positioned between

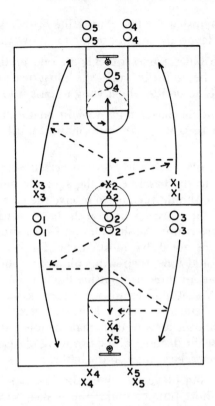

Diagram 6-5. Straight Line Break Against Two Defenders

three offensive players who are in a straight line such as X_3 O_2 X_1 O_1 X_2, can easily be defended.

Following these two lead-up drills, our favorite 3-on-2 half-court and full-court drills are executed according to the following rules and checklists that are given to our players.

PROPER EXECUTION FOR
3-ON-2 SITUATIONS

The basic set for going down the floor on a fast-breaking three-on-two situation is a triangle with the ball in the middle. The offense would first like to score with a short jumper under the basket. The second option would be a well-balanced and controlled jump shot off of the free throw line.

Checklist: Offensive Player

1. The girl with the ball must again make the defense pick her up. If the defense splits, she puts up a short

jumper inside the free throw line or drives in for a power layup if she can execute the move forcefully.

2. The dribbler passes quickly to one of the wings when she is picked up. She must read the back defender to decide which wing to pass it to.

3. The middle player must remain on the free throw line to keep the triangle formation until a shot is put up.

4. A wing player should position herself with her foot closest to the baseline on the square alongside the key. She should prepare to receive the pass and will use the same pivot action on the baseline foot as she did in executing the shot off of a 2-on-1 situation. (It should be noted that most coaches for men's basketball would have their wing players position themselves about three feet outside the lane on each side of the basket in order to create a greater area for the back defender to cover. However, female athletes lack the quickness of their male counterparts, so we decrease the distance of the two wing players to position themselves closer to the basket.)

5. If the wing player receiving the first pass does not get a short jumper under the basket, she quickly passes it to the other wing who has established position under the basket.

6. Knowing that everyone defends a three-on-two situation out of a tandem set (one behind the other), with the back defender taking the first pass and the top defender sliding down to stop the pass across the key, the wing player opposite the first pass steps across the lane with her foot closest to the free throw line to catch the defender on her hip and, thus, keep her in back of her. The offensive player gives a target away from the defender for a bounce pass.

7. If this wing player does not receive the pass, she is in excellent position for a rebound if she has stepped in properly.

Checklist: Defensive Player

1. When confronted with a 3-on-2 disadvantage, the defensive players must play a tandem.

2. The drive must be stopped *first* by the top defender.

3. When the pass goes to the wing, the bottom defender moves over to defend the shot.

4. The top girl shifts down to stop the pass across the lane to the other wing. She must move quickly and fight for position to keep from getting blocked out of the action.

5. If the pass goes back to the girl at the free throw line, one of the defenders makes a defensive fake toward her, but both guards are mainly responsible for holding their rebound positions.

Our favorite half-court 3-on-2 drill is also played with a chaser as was our 2-on-1 drill (see Diagram 6-6). For this drill, the ball is in the middle line. When the coach blows the whistle, the three offensive players in lines one, two, and three move toward the basket in triangular formation, with the dribbler in the middle lane. A player running with-

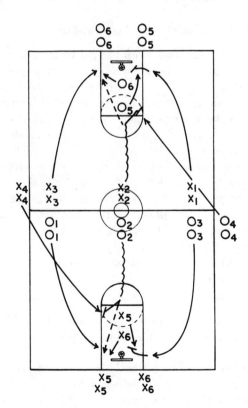

Diagram 6-6. Three-on-Two Drill with a Chaser

out the ball should be able to outrun a player dribbling; so when the dribbler approaches the free throw line, the wings should have already positioned themselves on the squares on opposite sides of the basket.

The players execute offensively and defensively according to the checklists. They are allowed only two passes, as it is our philosophy that there is time for only two passes on a 3-on-2 situation. The chaser will try to stop the pass back to the middle player; so staying in the free throw area, she must try to keep the defender behind her—as she would if she were blocking out in order to receive a pass back out, if it is necessary, and to maintain good rebound position. Players rotate from line one to line two to three to four to five to six and back to one. Line six plays the top defender position.

One point is awarded for each basket. X is the red team and O is the blue team. At the end of five minutes, the losing team will have to run. During the course of the drill, if the offense did not score, they must sprint to the opposite wall of the gym before rotating. This stipulation should be enforced only if there are enough players involved in the drill to assure fluid rotation.

Three-on-One Converted into Two-on-One

Three-on-one situations should be converted into two-on-one situations, because on a two-on-one situation, players should always get a layup or a jump shot right under the basket. If the players come down the court in a triangle formation against one defender, they could be forced to shoot a short jumper inside the key. Although a short jumper is also a high percentage shot, it is not as patented a shot as the layup or jumper right under the basket. This can be practiced using the same rules and formation that were described for the three-on-two drill, except that there now is a single defender under the basket. Seeing only one defender in the key, the dribbler will take the ball down either side of the lane. This signals the wing player on that side of the lane to "pop out to the corner" and then "V" cut to the middle of the key for rebound position (see Diagram 6-7). Once the ball is taken to the side, the same rules governing execution of a 2-on-1 situation go into effect.

Four-on-Two Drill

Our favorite four-on-two drill is a full-court drill that teaches the "trailer" (fourth player coming down the court on a fast break) her responsibilities.

The drill begins with X (the blue team) having the ball at midcourt. The coach blows the whistle and the blue team goes down the court in triangle with a trailer formation. The trailer stays behind the dribbler in the middle lane and approximately 12 feet away from her. When the middle player passes the ball to one of the wing players, the

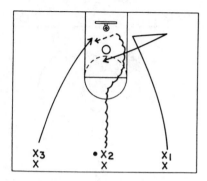

Diagram 6-7. Three-on-One Converted into Two-on-One

trailer fakes opposite the ball and then slides right around the middle player into the key looking for a pass from the wing player. Once the ball is shot or touched by a defensive player, the two players at the outlet positions may come in to help their teammates. If the shot is made, the ball is passed in from under the basket by the red team. The blue team guards them until mid-court. Once they pass mid-court, the red team tries to score against Y (the yellow team) using the same triangle with trailer formation. Should the yellow team gain possession of the ball on a missed shot, they quickly outlet the ball and try to fast break down the floor to score against the blue team.

The drill continues non-stop for eight minutes. Each basket counts one point. Since there are three teams, yellow's score will be kept on the visitor side, blue's score will be kept on the decimal digit under Home, and red's score will be kept on the unit digit under Home. The losing teams will have to run at the end of the drill.

Four-on-Three Drill

The same drill formation and rules may be used for this drill, but the points of execution will be slightly different. Seeing three players in the key signals the wing players to "pop out" to the corners for a pass (see Diagram 6-8). Should X_1 pass to X_2, X_4 (the trailer) follows the same rule of faking opposite and then sliding down to the post on the right side of the key. X_1 steps toward the ball right behind X_4's cut. Should X_1 get the ball, she can shoot the jumper or pass quickly to X_3 who is often wide open under the basket. If the pass does not go in to either X_1 or X_4, X_3 moves up the left side of the key looking for a crisp across-the-lane pass for a weakside power layup (see Diagram 6-9).

PENETRATION

The rules of execution on a penetration mismatch will vary with the different offensive philosophies of each team. The penetration situa-

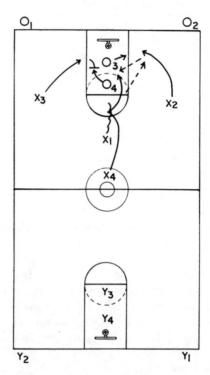

Diagram 6-8. Four-on-Two Drill

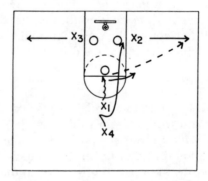

Diagram 6-9. Four-on-Three Drill

tions that we most often create and the drills we use to teach how to most effectively take advantage of them are as follows:

Punching the Gaps of the Middle Lane

One of our favorite methods of attacking zone defenses is to use a one-guard offensive set against a two-player front, and a two-guard

offensive set against a one-player front zone. Our first option against a
2-3 or 2-1-2 zone is created by having the point guard penetrate the gap
between the two top defenders (see Diagram 6-10). If she can make two
players pick her up, then, just for an instant, there is a four-on-three
situation. To penetrate the gap, X_1 uses a crab dribble. Turning sideways so that one shoulder is pointing toward the basket, the player, as
she shuffles, dribbles the basketball right between her knees with her
right hand if her left foot is the lead foot. She may pass the ball to either
wing player by using a crossover move to free herself after having established position between the two defenders. If the pass goes to X_2, X_3
flashes into the middle of the key. We try to hit her with a pass for a
short jumper if the middle defender has vacated her spot to defend the
shot (see Diagram 6-11).

If the weakside defender steps up to stop the flash, we can "alley
oop" to the weakside post as the weakside defender is pinned by X_3
using a reverse pivot roll cut through the lane. As the passing angle is
usually taken away by a tall middle defender for this weakside alley oop
option, we often find more success in the strongside alley oop option to

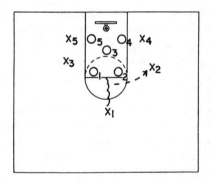

Diagram 6-10. Penetration Against a Two-Three Zone

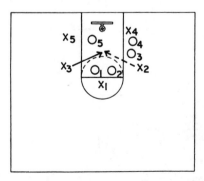

Diagram 6-11. Flash Option Against a Two-Three Zone

X_3 as she passes behind the strongside post. These alley oop options, of course, require good height and good jumping ability, not to mention excellent timing on the pass. We have often had the good fortune of having such personnel at the wing position, but when we didn't, we moved our most talented post player into the wing position for this particular attack.

We have two drills to practice the proper execution for these options—the flash drill and the alley oop drill. The flash drill is a three-player drill with X_1 penetrating the middle, passing to X_2 or X_3, with the weakside wing flashing to the middle or using a reverse pivot roll cut to go behind the middle defender to establish rebound position. X_2 may pass or shoot only after penetrating to the free throw line. The wings can only pass to the opposite wing or shoot the ball. They are not allowed to dribble.

Five minutes are put on the clock. Each basket counts as one point. The red team plays offense for two and one-half minutes and blue plays defense. They change assignments for the last half of the drill. The losing team has to run at the end of the drill (see Diagram 6-12).

In the "alley oop" drill, the coach may pass the ball to either wing. The wing player receiving the pass must read the shift in the defense (see Diagrams 6-13 and 6-14) to know whether to "alley oop" the pass to the weakside post or weakside wing, or whether to go directly to the strongside post if her man steps up to defend the wing. On this option, the strongside post, X_4, must step up the lane to keep the weakside post defender behind her on the shift. If there is no defensive shift on the pass to the wing, she may shoot the ball. There is no dribbling allowed except on a power move to the basket by the strongside post should she receive the ball to the wing. The same time allotment and scoring as described in the flash drill are used in this drill.

The gaps in the middle lane of an odd-front zone are on either side of the point defender. The dribbler approaches the gap from the side lane, once again using a crab dribble approach with her back to the

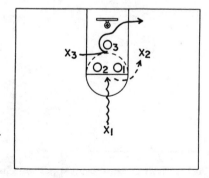

Diagram 6-12. Flash Drill

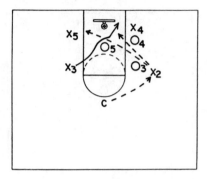

Diagram 6-13. Alley Oop Pass to Weakside Wing or Weakside Post

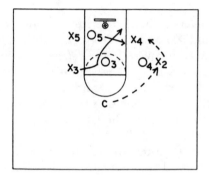

Diagram 6-14. Pass to Strongside Post

sideline (see Diagram 6-15). With this approach, she is facing all the offensive players except for the baseline player whom she can see out of the corner of her eye. Once again, her responsibility is to make two people pick her up.

Four avenues for passing the ball must be considered by the point guard in order to read the defense effectively. This is so that the point guard may take advantage of the mismatch situation that has been created by the punching action. The most frequently open avenue is a bounce pass to X_2 who has the option of shooting a jump shot from the free throw line, or passing to one of the post players or the baseline player depending on the defensive coverage. The second most likely open avenue is a sharp overhead pass or a reverse pivot bounce pass out of the double team to the baseline player who has the option of shooting a short jumper, passing the ball in to the strongside post or weakside guard depending on the defensive coverage, or penetrating from the side.

We practice these penetrating, passing, and shooting options in what we call our five-on-four diamond drill. The defense positions themselves in a diamond formation. If the coach calls out "Low," this refers to low coverage or taking away the baseline pass. If the coach calls

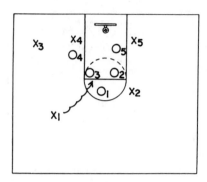

Diagram 6-15. Penetration of Middle Lane Gap of Odd-Front Zone

out "High," this refers to high coverage. On low coverage, O_4 fills the gap between X_3 and X_4, and O_2 drops into the middle of the key (see Diagram 6-16). On high coverage, the defense stays in the diamond formation until the pass is made. Five minutes are put on the clock. The red team, X, is on offense for two and one-half minutes, penetrating from both sides of the key. One point is awarded for each basket. The blue team, O, plays offense for the last two and one-half minutes. The losers run at the end of the drill.

The lob passes required in passing the ball down the last two avenues, possibly created by the penetrating action of the middle gap against an odd-front zone, are practiced in a double post drill which will be discussed in Chapter 7.

Penetration of the Middle Lane Against a Man Defense

We practice the penetration and "dumping" action of our penetration against a man-for-man defense from two basic drills. The first one is a three-on-three drill called rotation because of the defensive shifts (see

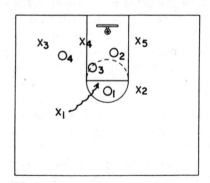

Diagram 6-16. Five-on-Four Diamond Drill

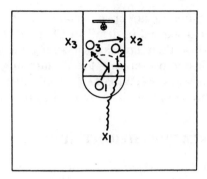

Diagram 6-17. Rotation Drill

Diagram 6-17). The point guard is influenced by the defensive stance of O_1 to either penetrate right or left. When O_2 steps up to stop the drive, O_3 shifts over to cover X_2 and O_1 drops down to cover X_3. Once again, five minutes are placed on the clock with each team playing offense for two and one-half minutes. One point is awarded for each basket with the losers running at the end of the drill.

Our 1-4 penetration drill is practiced out of a double high post set with two wing players free throw line extended. As the point guard begins penetration, the two post players slide down the key to the squares and the two wing players float to the baseline and then make a sharp cut back toward the free throw line (see Diagram 6-18). Penetration is once again influenced to one side or the other. As the post player, O_5, comes up to stop the drive, the opposite post, O_4, slides across the key to stop the pass to the strongside post, and O_3, the wing defender, steps in to stop the pass to the post on the weakside. The original point defender will shift over to cover the open wing player. Just for an instant, however, the wing player should be open. She has the option of shooting a

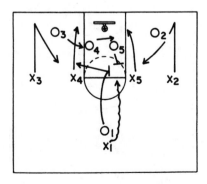

Diagram 6-18. One-Four Man Penetration Drill

quick jumper, passing to an open teammate, or penetrating. (Wing penetration will be discussed in detail in Chapter 12.) The post players are encouraged to use their bodies in blocking off the defensive shifts and thereby gain inside positioning for a "dumping off" action by the point guard or wing player. The same time allotment and rules governing the three-on-three rotation drill are used in this drill.

CREATING HEIGHT ADVANTAGES

Unfortunately, in 15 years of coaching, I have never had the pleasure of coaching a dominant-tall player. I have been fortunate, however, in occasionally having tall wing players and versatile point guards, which are necessary ingredients in creating a mismatch height situation.

We run an offensive pattern called "guard cut" which is ideally suited for posting up the point guard at the low post position. Instead of clearing the lane with the high post sliding down behind the screening action of the cut, the point guard comes back to the low post position and "shapes up" asking for the ball (see Diagram 6-19).

We teach all our players the three basic post moves and have them work on them in our daily form shooting drills. We also have all our players, regardless of their position, practice their post-defensive play in our MWF drill, called "defending the double post." Many coaches never talk about post-defensive play to their point defenders, much less practice it on a regular basis. However, it is an area that should always be checked out early in the game and exploited if it is found to be a weakness. For example, if there is a definite mismatch, such as a 5'8" point guard defended by a 5'3" player, the ploy of posting up the point guard will almost always prove to be productive and cause a team to make some reluctant defensive adjustments. We do not have a specific drill for this plan of attack; but as we are working on our half-

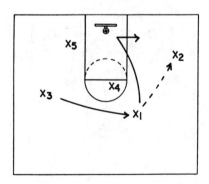

Diagram 6-19. Guard Post

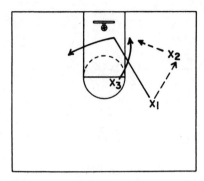

Diagram 6-20

court offense, whenever the coach calls out "Guard post," it signals the point guard to slip into the post.

Crossing action often forces defenders to switch defensive assignments. We use this tactic in our guard cut offensive pattern (see Diagram 6-20). Following the pass to the wing, the guard cuts through the lane and the high post crosses right behind her looking for a pass from the wing. This crossing action can create a natural screen for the post player. The defense will most likely try to prevent this by taking a denial stance that will not allow the high post player to slide down the key. But by faking the crossing action and then using a quick reverse pivot, the high post player should be able to pin her defender on her hip and ask for the lob pass, leaving only the point defender between her and the basket. The height mismatch should result in an easy jumper over the short defender, (see Diagram 6-21).

We practice these two options out of a three-on-three drill as diagrammed above. Five minutes are put on the clock with each team playing offense for two and one-half minutes. One point is awarded per basket, with the losing team having to run at the end of the drill.

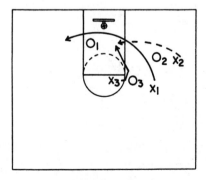

Diagram 6-21

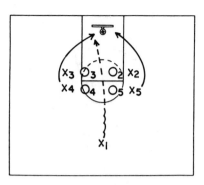

Diagram 6-22. Float

We have a series of set plays off a 1-4 stack set. They are practiced daily without the defense at the beginning of our after-school workouts. These plays rely on crossing and screening techniques to create a situation where a tall offensive player is guarded by a short one. Our favorite is called "float." When the point guard reaches a certain spot on the floor, she calls out "Break!" signaling the post players to "peel off" the stack to the basket (see Diagram 6-22). This causes the post defenders to be screened off by their own wing defenders. A high "alley oop" pass allows the post players to out jump the wing defenders and put the ball up right underneath the basket.

After having successfully pulled off the float play, the next time down the floor, the posts fake the "peel off" (see Diagram 6-23). Then one post player and one wing player "pop out" to the wing position. The ball is passed to the post at the wing. The strongside wing goes down to screen for the weakside post, thus screening off the tall defender. The ball is passed to the post player for an easy basket.

A third play off this set has the wing players set low on the squares (see Diagram 6-24). The posts pop out to the wing positions. As the ball

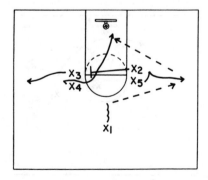

Diagram 6-23. Post

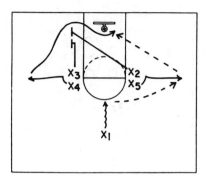

Diagram 6-24. Weak

is passed to one of the posts, the wings set a double screen to once again create a mismatch situation right under the basket.

These offensive plays, of course, work best as an element of surprise. We frequently use them in last-minute situations where the opponents are behind and are desperately trying to get back in the ball game by using a man-for-man defense as a last resort. A few easy buckets can totally demoralize a team trying to rally a comeback.

We drill these plays for two minutes a day, with two groups of five coming down the floor from mid-court—one group at a time. A manager standing outside the court along the baseline holds up a card that has the name of the play written on it, such as float, weak, post, etc. Any miscue in execution of the plays will cost that group of five a "half horse" at the end of the drill.

ATTACKING SPECIALTY DEFENSES

Even though I have never coached a dominant-tall player, I have had many outstanding players who simply could not be kept from scoring by conventional defenses. Therefore, it has become a standard practice to drill my teams against specialty defenses.

The most common specialty defense that we have encountered is the "Box and One." Our favorite method of attacking this defense is to create a mismatch situation by using screening and overloading tactics. X_3 is the best player for this. She pops out to the wing to receive the ball (see Diagram 6-25). X_1 cuts through the lane and establishes herself along the strongside baseline to overload that side of the floor. O_4 will most likely play the gap between X_4 and X_5, with O_2 shifting down into the middle of the key. X_5 comes up to screen for X_3 (see Diagram 6-26). As X_3 dribbles around the screen, she may shoot with the confidence of knowing that X_4 and X_5 have established good rebounding position. If O_4 steps up to help on the screen, X_3 fires the ball to X_1 who may shoot

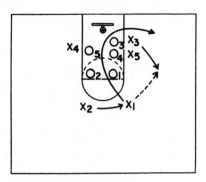

Diagram 6-25

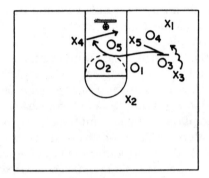

Diagram 6-26

the short baseline jumper or pass the ball in to X_4 who has established herself as the strongside post.

To practice this attack against the box and one, we put the clock on five minutes. The first team will be on offense against the second team for two and one-half minutes. Each basket scored counts one point. For the last two and one-half minutes, the second team and our best player, X_3, will be on offense, and the first team and one reserve will be on defense. The losing team, except for our best player who had to play offense the entire time, has to run at the end of the drill.

Our offensive attack against the "Diamond and One" defense is the same as was described for the "Box and One." The same rules and stipulations are in effect for this five-minute drill, except that the defense is in a diamond rather than a box formation.

A "Triangle and Two" defense is seldom used against our teams as we rarely have two outstanding scoring threats. We do, however, practice against it two or three times a week. Our favorite method of attacking the triangle and two zone is to simply take the two players who are being defended man-for-man out of the offensive set, and play three-on-three

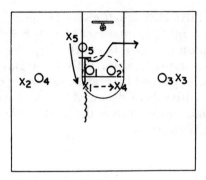

Diagram 6-27

with the three defenders in the zone. As we practice three-on-three sets every Tuesday and Thursday during our in-school workout sessions, we feel we can score consistently in every three-on-three situation with or without our best players being in the action. (These three-on-three sets will be described in detail in the next chapter.)

A brief description of how we apply the skills taught by these offensive sets to our triangle and two attack is as follows:

> The two players guarded man-for-man set up free throw line extended (see Diagram 6-27). Players X_2, X_4, and X_5 will run a screen-away series looking to score on a short jumper under the basket if the defense chooses to switch, or a jump shot from the free throw line should they try to stop the pass in under the basket (see Diagram 6-28). It should be noted that the two man-guarded players, X_1 and X_3, can try to get a backdoor when the open spot under the basket is on their side of the floor. If they do not get it, they move quickly back to their free throw line extended position.

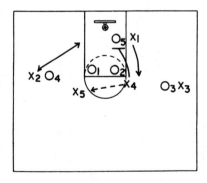

Diagram 6-28

Creating mismatch situations by fast breaking, penetrating, gaining a height advantage, or by simply having an outstanding scorer on the floor, is a fairly simple task. Capitalizing on these situations, however, calls for preparedness which can best be accomplished by practicing proper execution in the daily competitive drills described in this chapter, or those of similar design suited to meet the needs of your personnel and your team philosophy.

7

Competitive Drills to Teach Two-on-Two and Three-on-Three Offensive and Defensive Plays

We feel that there are certain fundamental offensive techniques that should be drilled on a regular basis to teach players how to become more potent offensive players. Therefore, we practice these techniques in competitive drills during our Tuesday and Thursday athletic period workouts. Although these drills were implemented into our program primarily to teach offensive prowess, we have also found them to be very beneficial to our defensive competency. Because we are known for our pressure man-for-man defensive play, many of these popular offensive techniques are frequently used against us. It is comforting to know that our players are well-versed in defending these techniques.

THE GIVE-AND-GO TECHNIQUE

The most fundamental offensive ploy in the game of basketball is probably the give-and-go technique. The drills that we use to practice this technique can be a 2-on-2 set or a 3-on-3 set. In our favorite drill, X_1 dribbles the ball to an area of the free throw line extended (see Diagram 7-1). X_2 fakes a backdoor and prepares to receive the ball on the opposite side of the free throw line. Upon receiving the ball, she quickly squares to the basket assuming a triple threat stance. X_1 fakes the backdoor and cuts to the basket over the top of her defender looking for a return pass from X_2. If she does not receive the pass inside the key, she clears the key area and maneuvers a series of backdoor fakes to get open for a pass from X_2, who takes her turn at the give-and-go option. These two players continue playing 2-on-2 until a basket is scored or until the defense gains possession of the ball through a steal, blocked shot, defensive rebound, or some type of miscue such as traveling or a lane violation.

This is a three-minute drill with the blue team, X, on offense and the red team, O, on defense for the first one and one-half minutes. The teams change from offense to defense and vice-versa for the last minute and a half of the drill. Each basket is tallied as one point on the scoreboard clock. The losing team will have to run at the end of the drill. During the course of the drill, if the offense fails to score, or if the defense is scored on, they have to run a sprint to the opposite end of the court and back without missing their turn. Players rotate from line one to two.

111

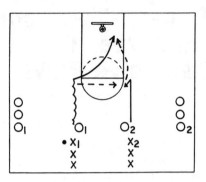

Diagram 7-1. Give-and-Go Drill

THE SCREEN-AND-ROLL TECHNIQUE

We use a 2-on-2 set in first introducing the screen-and-roll technique. In our first screening technique—the screen and roll off of the dribble—X_1 tries to drive the left side of the key (see Diagram 7-2). X_2 sets a screen for X_1 near the left side of the key. X_1 uses a change of direction to scrape off her defender on X_2. X_1 must read the defense to decide whether she should drive if the defense doesn't pick her up; whether to shoot a jumper if the defense picks her up, but sags to prevent a pass to X_2; or whether to pass the ball to X_2 rolling to the basket if she is open.

In the screen and roll with the dribble left drill, X_1 dribbles to an area near the free throw line. X_2 fakes the backdoor and then pops out to receive the pass. Upon receiving the pass, she immediately squares to the basket using the foot nearest the passer, X_1, as the pivot foot. In triple-threat position, she jab fakes left to keep her defender honest and preoccupied with stopping the drive, while X_1 comes over to screen her. Using X_1 as a screen, X_2 may drive right, shoot the jumper, or pass the ball in

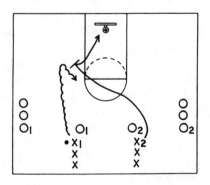

Diagram 7-2. Screen and Roll off the Dribble Drill

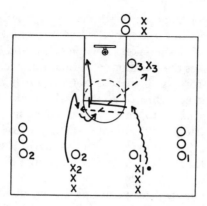

Diagram 7-3. Screen and Roll with the Dribble Left

to X_1 rolling to the basket according to what the defense will allow her to do. The jab, lean and go move should be used in driving the left side of the lane if the defense, in anticipating the screen, overplays to the right.

A third player is eventually introduced to these drills (see Diagram 7-3). Should X_2's defender move in to stop the drive or pass to X_1 rolling to the basket, X_3 must react accordingly and pass the ball to X_2. A third player may be added to the screen and roll off of the dribble in a similar fashion.

All of these drills are three-minute drills with the same stipulations for scoring and running as described for the give-and-go drill.

THE SCREEN AWAY DRILL

Screening away from the ball is a technique taught out of a three-on-three set (see Diagram 7-4). X_2, dribbling the ball from mid-court, can

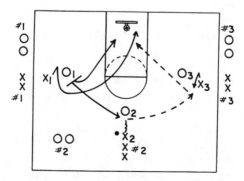

Diagram 7-4. Screen Away Without a "Switch" on Defense

pass the ball to either wing player who is faking a series of backdoor cuts to get open for a pass in the area of the free throw line extended. Should X_2 pass the ball to X_3, she fakes a give and go and then goes to set a screen for X_1. X_1 fakes the backdoor and then must read X_2's defender to utilize the screen properly. If there is not a "switch" (X_2's defender not picking her up), she goes directly to the basket looking for a return pass from X_3 who has squared to the basket and assumed triple-threat position. If there is a switch (see Diagram 7-5), X_1 goes toward the ball across the free throw line, thus allowing X_2 to roll across the key to the basket. X_3 must now read the defense in deciding whether to pass the ball to X_1 or X_2.

Players rotate to all three positions during this three-minute drill. Each team plays offense and defense for one and a half minutes. Each made basket counts as one point with the losing team having to run at the end of the drill. If there are enough players not to interrupt rotation, the coach may make the group of three not scoring or having been scored on run a sprint to the opposite end of the court before rotating.

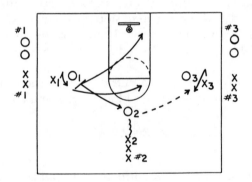

Diagram 7-5. Screen Away with a "Switch" on Defense

THE SPLIT-THE-POST DRILL

In the split-the-post drill, X_1 passes the ball to X_2 who keeps her back turned to the basket. X_1 fakes one way and then cuts to the basket, going either direction in an attempt to scrape her defender off X_2. X_2 hands off or pitches the ball to X_1 as she passes by. Or by looking over her shoulder at the defender behind her, she may fake the handoff and drive to the basket herself if her defender has stepped up to cover X_1 (see Diagram 7-6). This two-on-two drill is done in competition using the same time allotment, scoring system, rotation, and running stipulations described for the give-and-go drill.

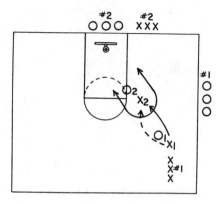

Diagram 7-6

THE WEAVE PLAY

The weave is a combination of all of the screen-and-roll techniques, including the split-the-post technique, which have been discussed in this chapter. X_1 may drive toward the basket in either direction (see Diagram 7-7). If she cannot get a layup or a short jumper, she continues her dribble directly to the spot previously occupied by X_2 or X_3. The wing players have faked the backdoor and have returned to their original positions. Now that X_1 is occupying X_2's spot on the wing, X_2 comes over the top of X_1 who has her back turned to the basket for the split-the-post option should X_2's defender choose to come over the top. If the defense chooses to go behind, X_1 pitches the ball to X_2. Upon receiving the ball, X_2 squares to the basket assuming triple threat position and reads the defense. X_1 may set a screen on X_2's defender for the screen-and-roll option (see Diagram 7-8). If nothing develops, X_2 continues her

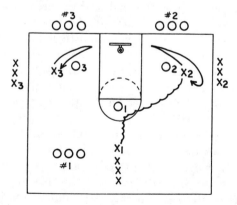

Diagram 7-7. Weave with Backdoor and Split-the-Post Option

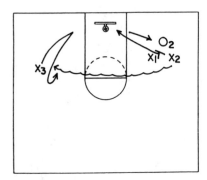

Diagram 7-8. Weave Pattern with Screen and Roll Option

dribble across the lane toward X_3. After rolling toward the basket, X_1 clears to the wing position opposite X_3. In the meantime, X_3, seeing the dribble advanced toward her, fakes the backdoor and then comes over the top of X_2 for the same split-the-post and screen-and-roll options that were available to X_1 and X_2 on the opposite wing. If nothing develops for X_3 and X_2, X_3 continues her dribble across the key toward X_1. Thus, a weave pattern is established. Once again, the same time allotment, scoring and rotation procedures, and running stipulations as described for the other drills are used.

The Five-Player Weave

This three-player weave pattern combined with the two-on-two screen and roll off the dribble technique can produce a potent five-player offensive attack. The basic set of this five-player weave is the double low post. The same rules governing the execution of the three-player weave and the screen-and-roll techniques apply to the proper execution of the five-player weave.

The post players follow these rules: If the drive is initiated toward your side of the court, you will clear to the low post position on the other side of the key. The post player opposite the drive would move to the high post area along the free throw line (see Diagram 7-9). On the dribble across the key by the wing player, the high post, X_4, should be used as a screener, as described in the screen and roll off the dribble drill. It should be noted that if X_5's defender should step in to stop the pass to X_4, X_2 would pass the ball in to X_5 who must step toward the ball to keep the wing defender, O_3, on her hip and out of the action (see Diagram 7-10). If nothing develops, X_2 continues her dribble toward the left side of the key. Once again the low post player, X_5, clears to the other side of the key. The high post player, X_4, who had rolled to the basket on the right side of the key, quickly steps out of the lane to avoid a

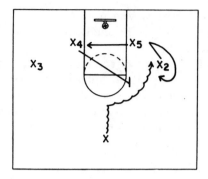

Diagram 7-9. Five-Player Weave Pattern

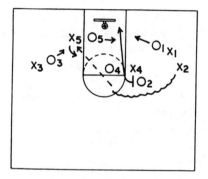

Diagram 7-10. Five-Player Weave Pattern with Screen off the Dribble Option

three-second lane violation and moves to the high post area along the left side of the free throw line for the screen off the dribble option, with X_3 on the left side of the key.

The weave is a potent offense if executed properly. The three outside players must be good ball handlers capable of reading the defense and executing the split-the-post and screen-and-roll techniques. The post players should be fairly mobile and also well-versed in executing the screen and roll off the dribble technique.

A great deal of discipline is required to run the weave effectively. It is a tedious offensive pattern designed to lull the defense into lapses of concentration by its continual weaving action. The players must have patience in its execution, and not try to force options which do not materialize.

The fact that the pattern is so tedious allows teams to use it as a delay tactic if running time off of the clock is desirable. It is also an excellent offense to utilize in the junior high school programs, as it develops good ball-handling skills and boosts team morale by its involvement of all five players.

This weave offense is practiced daily in our after-school practice sessions. How we apply the philosophy of competition to this type of half-court scrimmage situation work will be discussed in detail in Chapter 12. The purpose for our discussing the weave offense in this chapter is to show how our two-on-two and three-on-three offensive techniques can be meshed together to create five-player offenses, and how the regular drilling of these techniques can enhance our five-on-five game.

THE SINGLE-POST STACK DRILL

Utilizing the low post as a screen is still another screening technique which should be taught on a regular basis. Our favorite drill to teach this particular technique is the single-post stack drill in which X_2 stacks behind X_3. As the dribbler approaches, X_2 attempts to use X_3 as a screen. She may pop out to receive the ball on the wing and shoot over the screen; or, if her defender comes over the screen, she may loop X_3 and go to the basket (see Diagram 7-11).

This is also a three-minute drill with the blue team, X, on offense for the first minute and a half. Each basket scored is tallied as one point on the scoreboard clock. After a minute and a half, the red team, O, switches to offense. The losing team has to run at the end of the drill. Once again, during the course of the drill, if the offensive players fail to score or if the defensive players get scored on, the trio must run a sprint to the opposite end of the court. Players rotate from line 1 to 2 to 3 and back to 1.

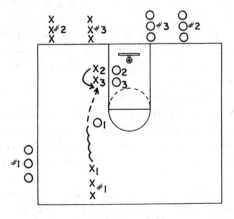

Diagram 7-11

THE DOUBLE-POST DRILL

We use this particular drill to teach our players the importance of starting the offense from a designated area of the floor, seeing the entire court by looking weakside, and using the lob pass effectively. In this drill, X_1 dribbles the ball to the spot designated by the enclosed square. We refer to this area as the "magic square," as we feel that our offense is most effective when the guard has penetrated into this area of the court before initiating the offense (see Diagram 7-12). X_1 must stare at X_3 to freeze her defender. Once she has reached the square and frozen X_3's defender, she lobs the ball to X_2, using the bottom left-hand corner of the backboard as a target. X_2 may shoot the ball, pass to X_3, or pass back out to X_1 depending on the defensive coverage. This three-minute drill follows the same rules for rotation, scoring, and running as described for the single-post stack drill.

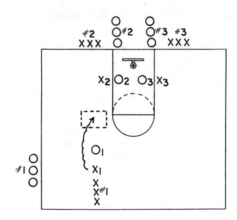

Diagram 7-12

THE TRIPLE-POST DRILL

The triple-post drill is designed to drill our players in low and high post skills, offensive rebounding positioning, and offensive cutting action techniques. In this three-on-three drill, the coach stands in an area with open passing lanes to X_1, X_2 or X_3. When he/she slaps the ball, this signals the defensive players, who must start the drill positioned behind the player they are guarding, to try to assume a fronting stance on the low post player and cover-out stances on the high post players (see Diagram 7-13). Should the ball be passed in to the low post player, the strongside high post, X_2, quickly moves to an area in the middle of the key just below the dotted line of the circle. She assumes a wide stance, trying to keep her defender behind her so that she is open for a

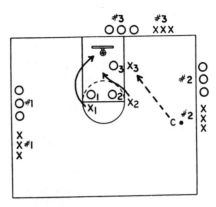

Diagram 7-13. Triple Post with Rebounding Positioning Assignments When Ball Is Passed in to the Low Post

pass from the low post or in excellent rebounding position. The weakside high post player, X_1, tries to beat her defender to a position under the basket opposite the ball, also assuming a wide stance to keep her defender behind her for the pass or rebounding. X_3 using one of the three low post moves either shoots the ball or dumps it off to X_2 or X_1.

Should the ball be passed in to the strongside high post, X_2, the other two post players fake a backdoor cut or a pop out to give X_2 time to pivot and square to the basket. The two cutting action rules that must be followed are: 1) the low post cuts first across the key, 2) the high post without the ball cuts diagonally, which provides a natural screen for the low post "looping" right back into the middle of the key behind the diagonal cut (see Diagram 7-14). The high post player with the ball must read the defense in deciding whether to pass the ball in or to use one of the three high post moves in trying to score. Regardless of the

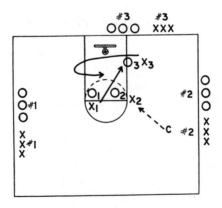

Diagram 7-14. Triple Post Cutting Action When the Ball Is Passed into the High Post Strongside

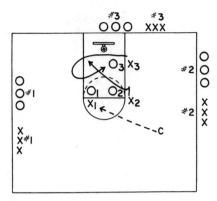

Diagram 7-15. Triple Post Cutting Action When Ball Is Passed into the Weakside Post

option she chooses to take, the players are to position themselves so that all three spots surrounding the basket are occupied for an offensive rebound.

Should the ball be passed in to the weakside high post, X_1, the same rules for proper execution described above are followed (see Diagram 7-15). This is also a three-minute drill with each team playing offense for one and a half minutes, and individual players rotating to all positions.

To encourage rebounding aggression further, scores are tallied on the scoreboard clock as follows: 1 point for a made basket; 1 point for an offensive rebound; and 2 points for a made rebound shot. At the end of the drill, the losing team has to run.

ZONE PENETRATION

To teach our players to penetrate, fake the shot if necessary, and dump off, we use a drill called the "mini game" (see Diagram 7-16). The defense plays a triangular zone defense within the lane. X_1 tries to penetrate until two defenders are forced to pick her up. X_2 and X_3 step into the open spots in the key created by the penetration and look for a dump off pass from X_1.

X_1 should use a head and shoulder fake to get the defense to put their hands up, so she can dump the ball off under them. She may have to shoot the ball to keep the defense honest. If neither X_2 or X_3 can receive the pass inside the key, they quickly pop out to receive the pass and then try to penetrate and dump from their respective positions.

A shot may be taken only inside the key. Three-second violations must be honored. This drill has the same time allotment, scoring and rotation procedures, and running stipulations as described for the screen-away drill.

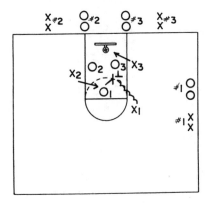

Diagram 7-16. Zone Penetration "Mini Game"

RULES FOR MAN-TO-MAN PRESSURE DEFENSE IN DEFENDING THESE TECHNIQUES

As stated in the beginning of this chapter, the above-described drills were implemented into our program primarily to improve our offensive game. We have, however, discovered our defensive play has been improved by these drills as they create many situations which we will face during the course of a season. A detailed explanation of how the various offensive techniques of these drills would be defended according to our philosophy would not only be lengthy, but repetitive of our defensive philosophy discussed in Chapter 5.

A list of rules which our players must follow in playing defense, not only in these drills but in scrimmage and game situations, are given as handouts to our players. An oral or written test with players having to run one suicide for each wrong answer is from time to time administered to the team. These rules were adapted for our program from Don Horn of Snook High School who for several years was one of the most successful boys' coaches in Texas. They are as follows:

1. Keep them pressed out of their pattern.

2. You are responsible for *your player, the ball,* and *the middle.*

3. Stay down low.

4. Use the heel-toe stance and shuffle when guarding the dribbler. Your arms should be straight and your hands should shake.

5. Don't press to the extent that your player penetrates or gets by you.

6. Don't reach for the ball if your body has to move. Keep your elbows inside of your knees.

7. Watch for the screen as you defend the dribbler. (You have to rely on the "eyes in the back of your head". . . your teammate.)

8. Try to force the dribbler off the screen.

9. There are four ways to defend a screen (listed in order of preference):
   a. Go over it . . . arm and leg first.
   b. Go behind it if the offense is not within shooting range.
   c. Help and recover.
   d. Switch.

10. If you are forced to switch:
    a. Try to get behind the screener and draw the charge as she rolls to the basket.
    b. Try to use the help and recover technique of helping stop the dribbler and then rolling with the screener to play the float pass. It may force the dribbler to throw an interception or at least take a farther distance, lower percentage shot.

11. Get tight when the dribbler stops. Jump up and down, waving hands, screaming "DEAD!" This signals everyone that the dribbler has picked up the ball and everyone is to cover-out tough.

12. Never raise up on defense except when fronting the post. (We always front when the ball goes to the wing and to the corner unless instructed otherwise.)

13. Deny every pass when the ball is one pass away. *Work hard on all girls away from the ball.*

14. The farther your player is from the ball, the farther you are away from your player. *Be ready to help out on the weakside.*

15. Don't let your player cut to the basket between you and the ball. Move in the direction the ball moves before your player does. "Step to the ball!"

16. If a pass comes to your player, you either "play the pass" or "defend the *point.*"

17. Use good judgment in playing the pass. Keep shuffling and stay in your cover-out stance. A deflection or interception can be made as easily as if you had opened up, and it is much safer in defending the backdoor. *Never allow the backdoor!*

18. Respect good passes.

19. Your head should not go up and down as you move when denying the pass. Use a wide stance to shuffle and drag the back foot.

20. Don't ever let your player receive the ball going to the basket. Always make her move away from the basket to receive the pass.

21. Don't allow contact unless you are in a good defensive stance and in good defensive position. Don't hook the offensive player with your arm, and don't get hung up on the player's backside. Move your feet.

22. When the ball goes into the low-post area (dribbled or passed), "belly up" and *ask for help only if you cannot contain the offensive player alone.*

23. Do not double team in the post area unless you see that your teammate needs help. Keep your girl from receiving the pass back out.

24. If a player gets loose and is going to the basket, the closest defender must pick her up. The girl, who lost her player in the first place, picks up the open offensive player (determined by the rotation of the defense).

25. Do not leave a girl in the post area and go out of the lane to pick up a loose player coming to the basket. Let her come to you.

26. Never leave the floor until the shooter's feet leave the floor. Try to put your hand on the ball to make them shoot higher.

27. Switch automatically in the back court on crosses where the ball is involved.

28. *React quickly after losing possession of the ball.* Find your girl.

29. Know where your player is when we are shooting a free throw.

30. Use the baseline and sideline as a helper.

31. Apply as much pressure as you possibly can with respect to your ability and the ability of the girl you are guarding. *No more; no less.*

32. Pressure defense is a *five player proposition.* We are as good as the weakest player on our team.

33. Stay ahead of the play. Don't trail behind the play like a "puppy dog."

34. Talk on defense. Talk to the opponents. It is distracting. Talk to your teammates. Make them aware of what is going on behind them.

8 Improving Rebounding Skills With Competitive Drills

During my fifteen-year coaching career, I have heard hundreds of clinic lectures and have seen many coaches dexterously draw up sophisticated offensive patterns. I could count on one hand, however, the number of lecturers who have supplemented their explanations of the options of a particular offense and who have made clear where the shots will likely come from, with the rebounding responsibilities of each probable shot selection. I refer to this method as "going one step farther after the shot goes up" in teaching an offensive set or pattern. In our program, we emphasize to our players that there is one more place each player has to go after the shot is taken before they start playing defense.

KNOWING WHEN THE SHOT GOES UP

Careful planning and preparation are the keys to good offensive rebounding. The factors to consider in this planning and preparation follow.

Shot Selection

This is perhaps one of the most difficult aspects of the game to teach. Some players simply seem to possess good court sense and always put the ball up at the right time. Other players hesitate to shoot the ball when they are open; still others "gun it up" even if they are swarmed by defenders. What is going on inside the players' minds has much to do with their shooting patterns.

Although most coaches are not psychologists, they need to try to identify each player's problem with her shot selection. We try the positive approach first. For instance, players who hesitate to shoot probably lack confidence or may even be fearful of being called a "ball hog." Lack of confidence is usually the result of simply not having spent enough time practicing. These are usually your "in-season" players. They seldom touch a basketball on their own, or they are always involved in a "pick-up" game. These players, who are not "natural" shooters, never spend enough time alone on a court to develop their shooting accuracy. Unfortunately, this lack of confidence in their shooting ability doesn't usually show itself until a team is well into the season.

Since high school players often don't have the extra time to practice shooting outside of the drill sessions, it seems pointless to tell a player that she should have practiced more in the summer or that she needs to practice more on her own. Besides, she is probably already feeling guilty enough, so it is better for the coach to take the approach that a missed shot is simply a pass to a fellow teammate.

We always tell our players never to be afraid of shooting the ball, since their well-versed teammates will no doubt get the rebound anyway. In addition, we never criticize a player for missing an outside shot as long as she follows these two rules:

1. On the perimeter, *never shoot over* a defender. You are to *maneuver around* the defense before taking the shot. If you are not open, don't take the shot. Exert patience, as there is a better shot awaiting the team.

2. *Never shoot* from the perimeter unless there are at least *three* players in an area near enough to the basket to cover the rebounding spots surrounding the basket.

Furthermore, we tell our under-confident shooters to fake confidence in putting up the shot, because if they don't, they will find themselves exactly in the position they are dreading. If they don't, the defense will sag off on them all night long. And if it comes down to the stall game, the player who has shown a lack of confidence in her shooting ability will most likely be fouled by the opposing team and forced to shoot free throws in a "do or die" situation. I've had several under-confident outside shooters who knew how to fake it so well that they were never put into an embarrassing situation by even the most alert defensive team.

Offensive Philosophy

There are several fundamental principles of our offensive philosophy that help our players establish offensive rebound position. For instance, since we are generally a post-oriented offensive team, our main objective is to get the ball in to the low post players. Once we have accomplished this, we expect the post player to put it up or to dump it off to someone inside. We always discourage a pass back out to a perimeter player from the low post position. This is because we feel that our chances of making a basket or being fouled are maximal in the low post area. Consequently, when the ball does go in to the low post, our players immediately move to their assigned rebound area. They do not hesitate, as there is no doubt in their minds that the ball is either going to be shot or dumped off to one of the inside rebounders.

Occasionally, a tough defensive double or triple team of the low post may force one of our low post players to throw it back out. Invariably, we commit a three-second violation because our other players have gone inside the key to establish rebound position. We feel that this is unavoidable, since the number of times that we score off of an offensive rebound far outweighs the number of times we lose possession of the ball because of a three-second violation.

Other offensive principles that signal our players that the ball is going to be shot are as follows:

1. Any rebound inside the key is put back up. We are not going to get any closer than we are at that instant, so players are expected to force it back up if necessary. Once again, we feel that our chances of making the basket or getting fouled are excellent. It would be futile to pass or dribble the ball back out only to set up and try to get the ball back into the low post area. The only time this is a reasonable alternative is when we are ahead and trying to use up as much time on the clock as possible.

2. As discussed in Chapter Six, in a two-on-one situation our players are allowed only one pass before taking the shot, and only two passes in a three-on-two situation. We feel that the defense would be breathing down our necks if it took more time to execute properly. Therefore, our players immediately move to establish rebound position after the allowed number of passes have been completed, because they know that the ball is going up.

3. Our wing players and our high post players are allowed only two dribbles toward the basket before having to either shoot the ball or pass off. More than two dribbles from these positions allows too much time for the defense to cover whatever options may have developed. Therefore, after two dribbles, the weakside players start heading toward their assigned rebound positions anticipating a shot. If there is a pass, they quickly pop out of the key to avoid a violation.

Player Evaluation Questionnaire

Several times during the year, we have our players evaluate one another in the form of a questionnaire. Our questionnaires vary from year to year to best suit our personnel; but an example of the questions which help our players become more familiar with one another's shooting habits are as follows:

1. Does <u>M A R Y</u> shoot a lot? Yes:_____ No:_____

2. What is her favorite spot to shoot from: _____

3. Are you confident in her ability to shoot from this position? Yes: _____ No: _____

4. Is her shot selection wise? Yes: _____ No: _____

5. How could she improve it? _____

6. Do you think she shoots: too much _____ not enough _____ only when the shot is there _____

Examples of questions dealing directly with offensive rebounding are as follows:

1. Is she a lazy rebounder? Yes: _____ No: _____

2. Do you trust her to be in position to get the rebound if you miss the shot? Yes: _____ No: _____

3. If she were to get paid $100 for each offensive rebound she got during practice or a game, do you think she would try harder? Yes: _____ No: _____

4. If she were responsible for floor balance when the shot went up, would you trust her to do so or would she go charging in for the rebound? trust her _____ go charging in without thinking _____

The results of the questionnaires are returned to each individual unsigned. The players are more likely to listen to the criticisms of their peers than they are to the coach; but equally important is their familiarization with one another's playing habits. Anticipation and predictability are important factors in establishing good offensive rebounding position.

REBOUNDING ASSIGNMENTS

There are five players on the court, and each player has a rebounding assignment to take care of when the ball is shot. First of all, the three spots surrounding the basket must be dealt with (see Diagram 8-1). We practice covering these spots in our Tuesday and Thursday offensive workout drills (see Chapters Seven and Twelve). As a general rule, the player closest to one of these three spots takes the shot. The shooter is to follow her shot if she is inside the key. Outside the key, she is to hold her floor position long enough to follow through properly. If a player is overly intent on following the shot, she often forms the bad habits of shooting off balance and not finishing the release with good follow-through. A helpful hint for shooters is to tell them that 90% of their missed shots will either come right back to them or will rebound directly opposite them on the other side of the court at the same angle it was shot. The player who is not the shooter and is not occupying one of the three spots under the basket is responsible for floor balance.

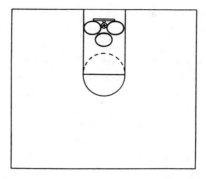

Diagram 8-1. Three Rebounding Spots Surrounding the Basket

FAKING

The offensive player is usually at a disadvantage when the ball is shot, as the defense will generally be between her and the basket. In order to get to one of the three spots under the basket, the offensive player must use some finesse—usually in the form of faking one direction and then going another. A good drill to teach offensive faking, as well as defensive concentration on the player instead of the flight of the ball, is blocking out.

Three minutes are put on the clock. The offensive team, X, is the blue team; the defensive team, O, is the red team. The first offensive player steps up to the free throw line facing the basket (see Diagram 8-2). The first defensive player takes a defensive stance between her and the basket, thus having her back to the coach who is standing under the

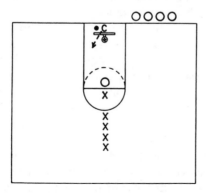

Diagram 8-2. Offensive Faking and Blocking Out Drill

basket with a ball in her hand. The coach will very slowly roll the ball toward one of the three spots under the basket. The offensive player is to fake out the defender and run and pick up the ball and shoot it. One point is awarded for each made basket. The defensive player is to block out the offensive player with a shuffle step and reverse pivot and then run forward to pick up the ball and hand it back to the coach. The players are encouraged to stay on their feet, as contact with another player's knees when diving for the ball could cause serious injury.

After the blue team has been on offense for one and a half minutes, they change places with the red team and play defense for the last minute and a half. At the end of three minutes, the losing team has to run.

PUTTING THE BALL BACK UP

Inside the key, we want our players putting the ball back up once they have gained control of a rebound. This requires daily practice in protecting the ball, squaring to the basket in a crowd, concentrating on making the shot in spite of the probable contact, etc.

Our favorite drill to practice putting the ball back up is called the "Killer Drill." We end our Monday, Wednesday, Friday defensive practice sessions with this drill. We have two players, one from the blue team and one from the red team, line up side by side in the lane. A third player starts off the drill by shooting the ball from the free throw line. The two players in the key fight to get the rebound and put it back up. Even if the shot is made, they grab it out of the net and put it back up. Make it or miss it, they are to keep rebounding and putting it back up for one minute. Should the ball rebound out of the key, the player retrieving the ball quickly throws it to the player on the free throw line who immediately puts it up again.

During this drill, a reasonable amount of contact is allowed. There will be leaning and shoving while jockeying for position. There will be hacking across the arms while the ball is being shot, etc.

The drill continues for one minute during which time each player counts the number of baskets she makes. At the end of the drill, the coach will ask each pair stationed at each of the six baskets in the gym, "Who won?" Each pair will reply, "Red, blue, or tied." The coach counts the number of wins by each team. Neither team is awarded a point if the score was tied at their basket. Should the red team have won at four baskets and the blue team at only two, the red team gets to go in while the blue team has to stay and run one suicide before going in. Should there be a tie, with say red winning at two baskets, blue winning at two baskets, and no points awarded at two of the baskets because of a tie, both teams would have to run.

TIPPING THE BALL UP OR OUT

Tipping Up

Each coach must decide for herself/himself whether players will be allowed to try to tip a rebound into the basket, or whether they should gain control of the rebound and then put the shot back up. My decision is based upon player strength, timing, and jumping ability. In my years of coaching, I have had only a handful of players whom I would allow to tip up a rebound. Because of the rare instances of having such personnel, a tip-up drill is generally not included in our workout schedule for the entire group.

Occasionally, however, a one minute full-court tip-up drill is used for purposes of conditioning (see Diagram 8-3). In this drill, the red team is on one court and the blue team is on the other. When the coach blows the whistle, player #1 of each line softly lays the ball up against the backboard and then runs the length of the court to the end of her team's line. The player behind her tips it up softly and follows player #1 to the other end of the court. Each player follows the player in front of them until all of the players are involved.

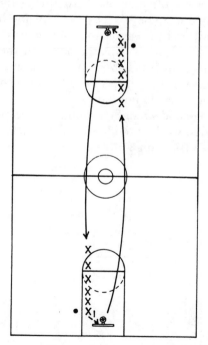

Diagram 8-3. Full-Court Tip Up Conditioning Drill

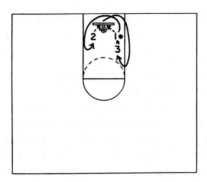

Diagram 8-4. Three-Man Tip Up Drill

Each time a team's ball hits the floor, the team is awarded a "negative" point on the scoreboard clock. At the end of the drill, the team with the most points is declared the loser and has to run; thus the term "negative" points was created. Sometimes we tell our players that if the ball hits the floor three times or less, neither team will have to run.

We also have a three player tip-up drill that is used by the three players most likely to be given the "go ahead" in tipping the ball in (see Diagram 8-4). Player #1 softly shoots the ball over the rim against the backboard and runs under the basket to get in line behind player #2. Player #2 tips the ball over the basket and runs under the basket to get in line behind player #3. Player #3 tips the ball over the basket and runs under the basket to get in line behind player #1, etc. The drill is performed for one minute. If the players have less than three "misses" (the ball hitting the floor), they do not have to run.

Players showing good strength, timing, and jumping ability in this drill will be allowed to work individually on an alley oop and an off the board tip-in drill (see Diagram 8-5).

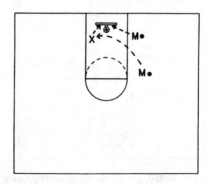

Diagram 8-5. Individual "Alley Oop" and Off-the-Board Tip Up Drill

For this drill, a manager throws an "alley oop" pass into the air just left of the basket. X jumps into the air and tries to tip it into the basket. Moving much closer in toward the basket, the manager softly shoots the ball up against the backboard. X jumps into the air and attempts to tip it into the basket. They work both sides of the basket. If X can get to where she is consistently tipping in three in a row, she usually has my permission to attempt tip-ins during our scrimmage sessions and drills. This is her final critique. If I feel confident in her ability to tip-in successfully, she will be given the go ahead to try it in game situations.

Tipping Out

All of our players are encouraged to try to tip the ball out. If a player sees that she cannot get "clean" control of a rebound, we tell her to keep the ball alive by tipping it up into the air. This may give her another chance to gain possession. If she sees that she can't get clean control of the rebound but she is aware of a teammate nearby, she may tip the ball out to her. We practice this in a "tip-out" drill (see Diagram 8-6).

For this drill, the blue team, X, lines up on one side of the circle, and the red team, O, lines up on the other side. The coach, standing in the middle of the circle, bounces the ball on the floor as hard as she can causing it to go high in the air. When the ball hits the floor, the first player in each line takes a giant step into the lane and tries to tip the ball out to her teammate standing next in line. Players should line up opposite next to someone their own height. The team having the most successful tip-outs, which are tallied on the scoreboard clock at the end of this two-minute drill, wins. The losing team has to run.

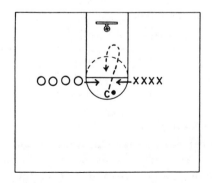

Diagram 8-6. "Tip Out" Drill

BLOCKING OUT TECHNIQUES

Blocking Out the Shooter

Blocking out is a term that goes hand in hand with rebounding. It refers to the technique of keeping the offensive player behind the defensive player, so that she will have the advantage rebounding. Different techniques must be used in blocking out offensive players according to their position on the floor if a team, such as ours, plays a denial defense. Therefore, different drills must be designed to practice the various blocking out techniques.

When the ball is shot, the defensive player is normally positioned between the shooter and the basket, so she is in excellent position to get the rebound if she blocks out correctly. In our one-on-one faking and blocking out drill, the defensive players learn to watch the player they are guarding instead of watching the flight of the shot. We tell our players that if the shooter makes a move toward the basket, they are to take one shuffle step to block her way and then use a quick reverse pivot in the direction the shooter is going. This keeps the offensive player blocked out with a minimal amount of contact. The defender should bring her arms up shoulder high and keep her elbows out, to provide a large obstacle for the offensive player to have to move around. The defender's hands should be spread wide toward the basket, so that she is ready to "snag" the ball.

Although the faking and blocking out drill described earlier in this chapter is excellent as a lead-up drill to blocking out the shooter, players need to practice defending a player who actually shoots the ball in order to learn how to become truly oblivious of the flight of the ball as it is shot. Our favorite drill to teach both aggressiveness and concentration in blocking out the shooter is called the two-man in the hole blocking out drill (see Diagram 8-7).

For this drill, two players are positioned under the basket. Red on one end; blue on the other. A red offensive line and a blue offensive line are positioned at mid-court facing their respective baskets. Player #1 from each offensive line dribbles toward the basket. She may shoot the ball anywhere outside of the key, but no lower than the second hash mark below the free throw line extended, as indicated in the diagram. One of the defensive players has stepped into the key where she must remain until the ball is shot. She can put her hands up to distract the shooter, but she cannot try to block the shot by leaving the key. The shooter will try to rebound her shot. The defender in the lane must be so tough in blocking her out that the ball must hit the floor first and then the defensive player may grab it. This is a minute and a half drill.

The offensive players get one point for making a basket outside of

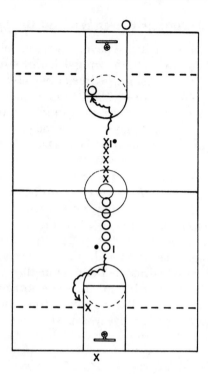

Diagram 8-7. Two-Man in the Hole Blocking Out Drill

the key on the first shot. Should they get the rebound and put it back up, they get two points put up on the scoreboard clock for their team. Should the second shot go in, a total of three points is awarded; two for getting the rebound and putting it back up, and one for making it. Should the offense get the rebound for a second shot, the defender must sprint to the other end of the court and back while the other defensive player is taking her turn. An offensive player failing to score must sprint to the other end and back.

Each of the two defensive players under each basket must block out successfully three times in a row. (A made shot outside of the key does not count as the defender's failure to block out. The count continues as long as the offense does not get a rebound.) Should either one of the two fail to block out three times in a row during the minute and a half drill, they each must run one horse. At the end of the minute and a half, two offensive players take their turn at blocking out. After all players have had their turn playing defense, the drill ends with the team scoring the least offensive points having to run a suicide.

Blocking Out the Perimeter Player Without the Ball

Because of the denial stance of having one arm and one leg between the offensive player and the ball, the wing defender must realize that the most open avenue to the basket for perimeter players without the ball is the backdoor route. They must be ready to take one shuffle step backward to defend the backdoor cut and then quickly reverse pivot on the back foot to keep the offensive player behind them.

We teach this in a two-on-two drill (see Diagram 8-8). The red team plays defense on one end and offense on the other, as does the blue team. The offensive player #1 dribbles toward the basket and shoots the ball following the same restrictions as described in the two-man in the hold blocking out drill. The defensive player, #3, must stay in the key as described in the previous drill. Player #4 assumes a defensive coverout stance on the wing player #2, and is responsible for blocking her out after #1 takes the shot. Players #3 and #4 must once again block out so tough that the ball actually hits the floor before they grab it up.

This is a five-minute drill with the same scoring as described for the two-man in the hole drill. Players rotate from line #1 to #2 to #3 to #4 and back to #1 on their respective teams. At the end of the five-minute drill, the losing team has to run.

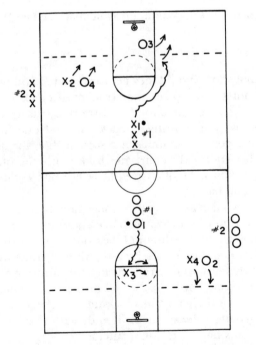

Diagram 8-8. Two-on-Two Blocking Out Drill

Blocking Out the Low Post Players When the Ball Is
Shot From the Middle

Once again, because of the denial stance of the post defenders when the ball is in the middle lane, an adjustment must be made to the blocking out technique. The low post players (as the wing players) will take the most accessible route to the basket to establish offensive rebounding position. The low post defenders, with one arm and one leg between their man and the ball, will have to use a quick reverse pivot on the foot closest to the baseline to keep their players behind them. There is very little room or time for the shuffle step with the offense set up so near the basket.

We teach this out of a three-man drill called the double low post blocking out drill (see Diagram 8-9). In this drill, X is the red team and O is the blue team. Player #1 dribbles to the free throw line and shoots according to the restrictions described in the last two drills. The defensive player #5 also follows the restrictions placed on her, as described in the two previous drills. Players #2 and #3 hit the offensive boards, while players #4 and #6 use the quick reverse pivot to block out these two low post players. The same time allotment, scoring system, and running procedures described for the two-on-two blocking out drill are used in

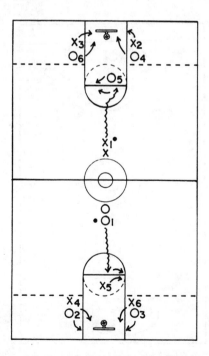

Diagram 8-9. Double Low Post Blocking Out Drill

this one. The defensive players, however, do not have to let the ball hit the ground before grabbing it up because the action takes place so close to the basket.

Blocking Out the Low Post Players When the Ball Is Shot From the Wing

According to our philosophy, when the ball is on the wing, the low post defender will front. Should the ball be shot, the defensive player who is fronting will find herself behind the post player. Therefore, we must rotate our post players to obtain inside rebound position.

We use a three-on-three drill to work on this rotation (see Diagram 8-10). A line is marked on the floor on the wing position. Player #1 dribbles up and shoots from behind the line. The defensive player, #4, must stay behind the line with her hands up until the ball is shot. She is then responsible for blocking out the shooter. The defender, #5, is fronting the low post player, #2, until the ball is shot. On the shot, she immediately takes off along the baseline and steps in front of player #3 to establish inside rebound position. Before the shot from the wing, the defender, #6, is playing between #2 and #3 in an open stance according to our philosophy of defending the double low post. When the ball is

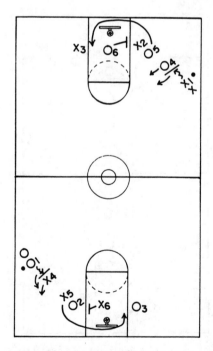

Diagram 8-10. Shot from the Wing Blocking Out Drill

shot, she comes across the lane to establish inside rebound position on player #2.

This is a five-minute drill with the same scoring and running procedures as described above. At the end of two and one half minutes, the ball is shot from the left side wing position.

Cross Blocking Out on the Free Throw

This rebounding trick was passed on to me by a coaching associate. We don't actually practice this in a competitive drill, but we do practice it regularly during our scrimmage sessions when we are shooting free throws.

For this drill, if I cross my arms, this signals my players to use this cross blocking out trick (see Diagram 8-11). When the ball leaves the shooter's hand, O_5 crosses the lane trying to get rebound position inside of X_4; O_4 crosses behind O_5 trying to get inside position on X_5; and O_3 fakes middle then slides down the side of the key, trying to get inside position under the left side of the basket.

It has often been said that the team that dominates the boards, dominates the game. Rebounding, along with pressure man-for-man defense and the fast break, are the three areas of emphasis in our program. It is a fundamental skill that may be learned at an early age, but the variety of techniques that arise because of various on-the-court situations must be drilled on a regular basis if your team is to truly dominate the boards.

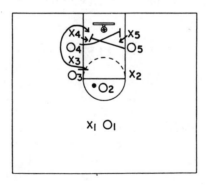

Diagram 8-11. Cross Blocking Out on the Free Throw

9 Improving The Fast Break With Competitive Drills

The fast break is another area of the game that is emphasized in our program. We feel that it fits well with our philosophy of pressure man-to-man defense, because a fast-breaking team puts constant pressure on the opposing team's defense. It is our philosophy to run the ball down the floor every time, if for no other reason than to test the other team's conditioning factor. If a scoring opportunity is available, we try to capitalize on it before the defense has had a chance to set up. If there are more than three players in the lane when the player leading our break hits the top of the circle, we pull up and play five-on-five.

Basic Principles and Lead-Up Activities

As was discussed in Chapter Six, the basic principle behind the fast break is to come down the floor quickly enough to outnumber the opponents momentarily and to take advantage of a mismatch situation, usually in the form of a 2-on-1 or 3-on-2 situation. The proper execution of these mismatch situations is discussed at length also in Chapter Six. It is improbable that a team can have an effective fast break without the mastery of execution of a 2-on-1 or 3-on-2 situation, so in teaching the fast break, the drills in Chapter Six should be used as lead-up activities to the drills presented in this chapter.

THE OUTLET PASS

Our first method of initiating the fast break is off of a missed shot. Proper execution of the outlet pass is all-important in determining how quickly the break can be initiated. We require the rebounder to turn in midair toward the sideline closest to her. Upon landing, the feet and body should be turned toward the outlet receiver. The pass should be a two-handed overhead pass. The ball is held above the head with the elbows slightly cocked. Rebounders must be careful not to bring the ball in back of their head where the opponents can get their hands on it.

We practice this outlet pass in what we call a one-minute Against-the-Wall Drill (see Diagram 9-1). The players get in pairs with one of the players standing with her back against a wall. On the coach's signal, she will throw a two-handed overhead pass from a standing still position to her partner, who is facing her and standing about 10 feet away on the baseline. Upon receiving the pass, X_2 will pass the ball back to X_1 using a chest pass and will take a giant step backwards, increasing the passing

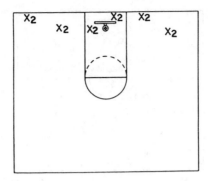

Diagram 9-1. Against-the-Wall Passing Drill

distance. The two players keep passing the ball back and forth, with X_1 using an overhead pass and X_2 using a chest pass. If the ball touches the floor before reaching the receiver or if it is dropped, X_2 must take a giant step forward. At the end of one minute, X_2 must be receiving the pass at a point even with the free throw line extended, or the pair has to run a half-horse. The partners then change positions with X_2 against the wall.

The purpose of this drill is to teach players how to throw the overhead pass without bringing it in back of their heads, as the wall will not allow them to do so. It also improves the sharpness and distance of the pass which are added benefits in unleashing a potent fast break.

Initiating the Fast Break

The next step to improving this outlet pass, and thus initiating the fast break more quickly, is adding the rebound and turn in midair to the pass itself. We practice this in a three-minute drill called Initiating the Fast Break (see Diagram 9-2).

For this drill, player #2 throws the ball underhanded against the backboard. Player #1 jumps as high as she can, rebounding the ball at the height of her jump, arms outstretched and fully extended to maximize her reach. Turning her body while still in the air, player #2 lands with her feet pointed toward her outlet receiver, player #6. Upon landing, or perhaps even before landing, she fires a two-handed overhead pass to the outlet receiver. The outlet receiver throws a baseball pass to player #4 who is running down the middle of the floor. Upon receiving the pass, player #4 dribbles with her right hand to the free throw line and bounce passes the ball to player #6, who has hustled down the floor in time to receive the pass and shoot a right-handed layup. Player #4 rebounds the ball and takes it with her to line #1, and prepares to throw the ball up against the backboard for player #3. Player #6 rotates to line #3, and player #1 rotates to line #2. As soon as the pass to the middle is

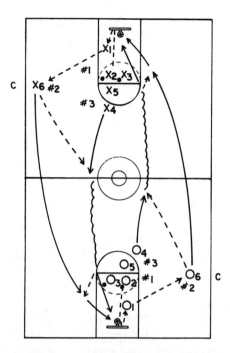

Diagram 9-2. "Break Out" Areas to Initiate Fast Break

completed, player #3 throws the ball up against the backboard for player #2 who rebounds, outlets, etc.

After one and one-half minutes, we change the drill to the other side of the basket, so that the players now outlet the ball to the other sideline, dribble with their left hand, and shoot a left-handed layup. While the blue team, X, is working on this drill on the left side of the basket, the red team, O, is working on the right side. A coach or manager positions herself along each side of the court even with the outlet player who is positioned free throw line extended. She is watching for proper execution of the outlet pass, the baseball pass, and the dribble, pass, and layup. If all parts of the drill are executed correctly by the team on her side of the court, the coach or manager will yell out "Point!" and one point is tallied for that team on the scoreboard clock. At the end of three minutes, the losing team will have to run.

LANE ASSIGNMENTS AND PLAYER RESPONSIBILITIES

We teach our players lane assignments and player responsibilities out of a two-three zone set (see Diagram 9-3). Gaining possession of the ball on a rebound, in fact, anticipation of gaining possession of the ball on a rebound, keys the other four players to "break out" to one of the four areas of the court marked on the diagram—low in the corners or

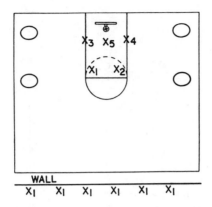

Diagram 9-3. Initiating the Fast Break

along the sideline free throw line extended. As the rebounder is turning in midair toward the closest sideline, her teammates are heading to the closest of these four spots. By breaking out this way, the defense has to spread out to cover them leaving the rebounder under the basket with one defender. If no outlet is available, she should be able to advance the ball up the court with a dribble. Our first option would, of course, be to outlet the pass to the outlet players free throw line extended. Our second option would be to outlet to one of the corner men; and our third option would be to have the rebounder dribble up the middle of the court. However, none of these things can develop if the players do not break out.

We practice this breaking out and lane assignment out of what we call a "Break Out Dummy Drill," meaning there is no defense. The coach standing at the free throw line will throw the ball up against the backboard (see Diagram 9-4). Should X_5 get the rebound, the other four players will break out to one of the four assigned areas. Should she outlet the ball to X_1, the opposite wing player, X_2, flashes to the middle looking for a pass. As she runs to the middle lane, she calls out "Middle!" The corner player opposite the outlet receiver, X_4, takes the left lane and hollers out "Left" while doing so. After passing the ball to X_2 in the middle, X_1 fills the right lane calling out "Right." The strongside corner player, X_3, moves to the middle lane behind X_2, shouting out "Trailer." The rebounder, X_5, fills the middle lane some distance behind the trailer and calls out "Safety." The group continues down the floor to the other end of the court where they mimic a four-on-two situation, executing according to the guidelines described in Chapter Six.

Should the ball go to X_3 on the rebound, the other four players once again break to one of the four "break out" areas. There is no set assignment as to who fills what spot, as long as all four are filled. Players once again call out their lane assignments and trailer and safety responsibilities (see Diagram 9-5).

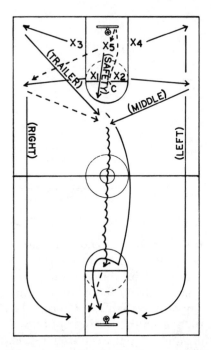

Diagram 9-4. Break Out Dummy Drill

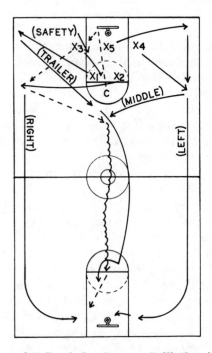

Diagram 9-5. Break Out Dummy Drill (Continued)

Some might call our fast break a "free lance," because we are not concerned with who fills what break-out spot or lane assignment, as long as they all get filled. This philosophy works best for us as in playing pressure man-for-man defense, as it is extremely difficult to predict the location of the defenders on the court when the ball is shot. Players must, therefore, be prepared to run from all positions on the floor.

It should be noted that should the rebound come to a player higher than the dotted line of the jump ball circle, the four "break out" spots are along the sideline free throw line extended and near the hash marks (see Diagram 9-6). It should also be noted on the same diagram, that if the ball cannot be passed in to the opposite wing player, X_4, she clears the middle lane and calls out "Right" for right lane responsibilities. X_5—who was going to assume the left lane assignment—seeing that X_4 did not receive the ball in the middle, flashes into the middle lane looking for the ball. X_3, who would have normally played the trailer role, must now hustle to the left lane. The outlet receiver, X_2, who anticipated taking the right lane, now must assume the trailer role. All of the players must call out their assignments.

This last maneuver is signaled by the coach who hollers out "Cross." This means that the first player coming into the middle could not receive the ball, so she must cross the middle lane and assume strongside lane responsibilities. X_1 remains the safety.

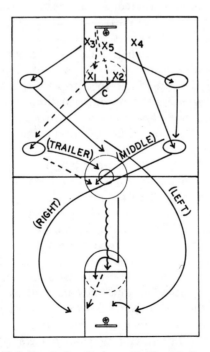

Diagram 9-6. Break Out Dummy Drill with Cross Option

This is a five-minute drill with the red team, X, and the blue team, O, taking turns. All players rotate to all positions. Teams are awarded one point each for proper execution by the coach who hollers out "Point," signaling the scorekeepers to tally one point on the scoreboard clock for the appropriate team. At the end of five minutes, the losing team runs a suicide.

This drill is later turned into a 4-on-2 drill. The blue team, O, positions two men in the lane in a tandem set to defend the approaching red team. They play 4-on-2, according to the rules described in Chapter Six. After the blue team gains possession of the ball, they line up in a two-three zone set and the coach or a manager throws the ball up for them. They rebound, break out, outlet, call out their lane assignments, and take the ball down the floor to the opposite end of the court where two red team players are waiting in a tandem set ready to defend their basket. The scoring differs only in that one point is awarded for proper execution and another point is awarded to the offensive team if they make the basket. At the end of the drill, the losing team must once again run.

Transition Drill

Our favorite fast break drill is a full-court 2-on-1 and 3-on-2 transition drill. Once all of the lead-up drills (described in Chapter Six and in this chapter) have been mastered, we are ready to introduce this drill which will become part of our daily workout (see Diagram 9-7).

For this drill, the red team, X, starts off with X_1 passing in the ball to X_2. With X_2 dribbling the ball, they move down the court to play 2-on-1 against the blue team's sole defender, O_1, positioned under the basket. Following the guidelines for proper execution that were described in Chapter Six for a two-on-one situation—such as one pass only and it must be a bounce pass—the red team tries to score. Should they make the basket, O_1 steps out of bounds immediately and fires in a pass to O_2 or O_3 who prepare to go down the court against the two red team players, X_1 and X_2. X_1 and X_2 must quickly transist from offense and race down to the other end of the court and set up in a tandem set, and prepare to defend the 3-on-2 onslaught.

It should be noted that had O_1 gained possession of the ball through a rebound, she would have quickly outleted the ball to O_2 or O_3, and they would once again have moved down the court hoping to capitalize on a 3-on-2 situation against the two red team players. Once X_1 or X_2 gains possession of the ball either through a rebound or a made basket, she quickly outlets or inbounds the ball to the next red team player in line #2. She and the next player in line #1 go down the floor looking to capitalize on a 2-on-1 situation against the next player of the blue team in line #1. The three blue team players, who had just come

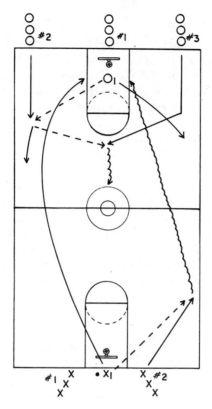

Diagram 9-7. Two-on-One and Three-on-Two Transition Drill

down the floor trying to score on a 3-on-2 situation, step off the court and run up the sideline back to their basket where they will rotate from line #1 to #2 to #3 and back to #1, so that they have the opportunity of playing all positions. The red team players rotate from line #1 to #2 and back to #1.

It should be noted that the guidelines described in Chapter Six for proper execution of a 3-on-2 situation—such as two passes only, stepping in to block the shift of the top defender, etc.—are to be followed. Special stipulations for this drill will have the players run a lap or a bleacher before rotating to their lines if they fail to score. The drill is a five-minute drill with the red team playing two-on-one the first two and a half minutes, and the blue team three-on-two. For the last two and a half minutes of the drill, blue tries to score two-on-one and red tries to score three-on-two. The team scoring the least amount of baskets, which are tallied on the scoreboard clock at one point each, has to run at the end of the drill.

Sideline Fast Break

Our second method of initiating the fast break is off of a missed or made free throw. To keep our opponents off balance, we frequently use a sideline break in this situation (see Diagram 9-8).

The basic principle behind this break is to try to pass the ball up the sideline quickly enough to capitalize on a 2-on-1 situation. If the shot is made, player #5 quickly steps out-of-bounds and fires a pass to player #2 who is free throw line extended.

It should be noted that all of the players who will be taking the sideline position should take the pass over their right shoulders, not only to protect it, but to be able to pass the ball more quickly down the sideline. We tell our players, who are planning to relay the ball up the sideline, that their toes must be pointing toward the sideline. Player #2 passes the ball to player #1 who is positioned just below the mid-court line. She in turn fires the ball to player #3, who must really hustle to position herself along the sideline free throw line extended on the other end of the court. Upon receiving the pass, players #3 and #4, who have taken the left lane assignment, try to score two-on-one.

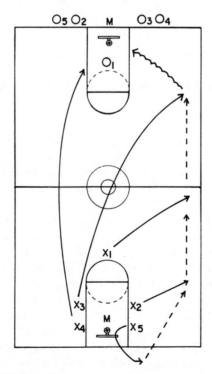

Diagram 9-8. Sideline Break off Made Shot with Two-on-One Option

We practice this 2-on-1 option of the sideline break by having the red team, O, put one defender in the lane, so that X_3 and X_4 must execute properly to score. It is then the red team's turn to practice the 2-on-1 option of the break against a sole blue defender. A manager shoots the free throw at each end to initiate the break. She stands in the middle of the key about three feet away from the basket, so that she is sure to make it for the first minute of the drill.

For the second minute of the drill, the manager shoots from the free throw line, so that we can practice the sideline break 2-on-1 option off of a missed shot (see Diagram 9-9). Should the rebound go to X_5, the break assignments remain the same except that they are run to the opposite sideline, and X_2 will now take the deep sideline assignment and try to score 2-on-1 with X_5. Should the rebound go to X_2 or X_3, the players all rotate one spot up (see Diagram 9-10). X_1 takes the free throw line extended position; X_3 positions herself near the mid-court line; X_4 hustles down the floor to assume the free throw line extended position on the opposite end of the court; and X_5 must fill the left lane of the court and prepare to play two-on-one with X_4.

For the next two minutes of the drill, we practice the 3-on-2 option

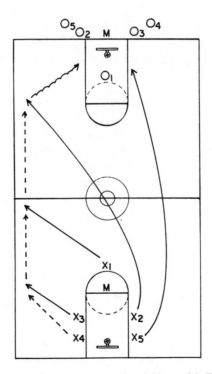

Diagram 9-9. Sideline Break off Missed Shot with Two-on-One Option

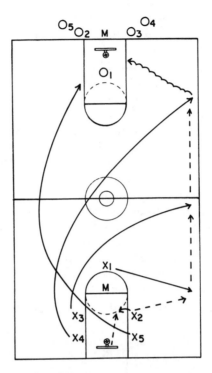

**Diagram 9-10. Sideline Break off Missed Shot with Two-on-One
Option (Continued)**

of the sideline break (see Diagram 9-11). Upon seeing two defensive
players in the lane, X_3 passes the ball to X_2 who has assumed the middle
lane assignment. X_2 tries to score 3-on-2 with players X_4 and X_3. X_1
assumes the trailer position, and the rebounder, X_5, is the safety. The
second 3-on-2 option of the sideline break is created when X_2 or X_3 is
forced to dribble to the middle lane because the sideline pass has been
taken away. The coach signals this dribble option during the drill by
shouting out "Dribble" (see Diagram 9-12). X_1 or X_2 dribbles the ball
into the middle trying to score three-on-two with X_3 and X_4, while X_1 or
X_2 assumes the trailer role and X_5 acts as the safety.

At the end of this four-minute drill, the losing team has to run.
Early in the season, points are awarded for proper execution—one point
per successful trip down the floor and one point for a made basket. Once
the execution has been mastered, points are awarded only for made
baskets.

Early Offense

A good fast-breaking team tries to score before all five players of the
opposing team can run down the court and set up their defense. In this
way, if a 2-on-1 or 3-on-2 situation does not develop, they can try to

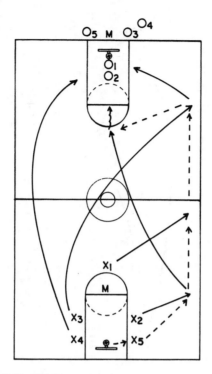

Diagram 9-11. Sideline Break with Three-on-Two Option

score three-on-three using one of the offensive techniques described in Chapter Seven.

We use the sideline fast break drill to practice our early offense techniques (see Diagram 9-13). As X_1 approaches the free throw line, seeing that there are three defensive players in the key, X_3 and X_4 pop out to the corner. X_1 can pass the ball to X_3 and then try the give and go option against her defender, thus sliding down the side of the key to the low post position. If this option is not available, the trailer, X_2, goes to the strongside high post position and X_4 moves to the weakside high post position. The corner player, X_3, may pass the ball to X_2 for a triple post cutting action, described in Chapter Seven (see Diagram 9-14). Upon receiving the ball, X_2 squares to the basket. According to the rules of the triple post cutting action drill, the low post cuts first, the weakside high post cuts diagonally, and the low post loops back into the key behind the natural screen of the diagonal cut.

The middle player leading the break may choose to use a screen away technique in setting up an early offensive attack (see Diagram 9-15). On passing the ball to X_3, X_1 fakes the give and go options and goes to screen for the opposite wing player, X_4, and then rolls across the key to the low post position. X_4 may use the screen and flash to the strongside high post position with the trailer, X_2, taking the weakside high

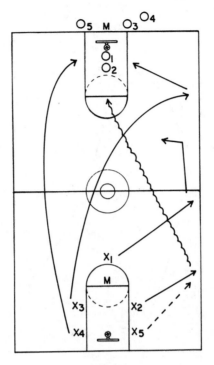

Diagram 9-12

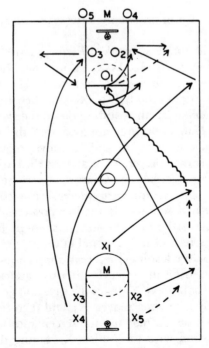

Diagram 9-13. Early Offense with Give and Go or Triple Post Option

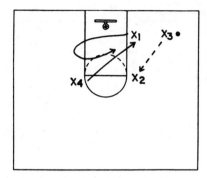

Diagram 9-14. Early Offense: Triple Post Cutting Action Option

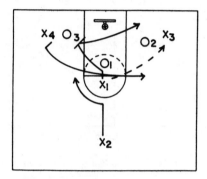

Diagram 9-15. Screen Away Option in Setting up the Early Offensive
Attack on the Triple Post

post position. Or the trailer may take the strongside high post position
signaling the weakside wing, X_4, to take the weakside high post position. If the ball does not go into the low post on the screen away option,
the corner player may pass the ball to the strongside, or even the weakside, post player to initiate the triple post cutting action.

Once the players have mastered these early offense techniques using
the sideline break drill as described in the previous drills, we add two
chasers along the baseline, so that the drill becomes more realistic—
convincing the offensive players that execution must be done quickly
and precisely (see Diagram 9-16).

We practice this drill for four minutes later in the season when all
of the other sideline break techniques have been mastered and no longer
need repetitive drilling. The teams take turns playing offense and
defense. One point is awarded per basket; one point is awarded if the
group runs the ball down the floor, goes through all of the early offense
options, but sets up in our triple post five-on-five set should nothing
develop; and the score goes back to zero if the offense forces an attempt
to score. The chasers may not leave the baseline until the ball crosses the

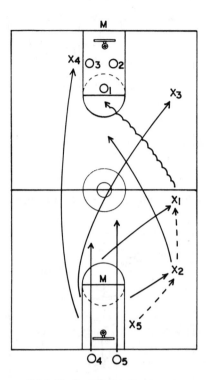

Diagram 9-16. Early Offense Drill with Chasers

mid-court line; but quite often a small miscue in execution allows them to get down the floor soon enough to foil a scoring opportunity. It is important that the coach not allow the players to force the fast break or early offense. Bad habits can be reinforced if coaches do not demand proper execution in this type of drill. As always, the losing team has to run at the end of the four-minute drill.

10

Developing the Press
With Competitive Drills

With as great a commitment as we make to pressure man-for-man defense, there is little time left for working on zone press principles. During our after-school workout sessions, however, 20 minutes are spent daily on *attacking* various presses rather than capitalizing on them defensively. To practice attacking zone presses effectively, it is necessary to teach trapping and gapping and rotation techniques, so that the defense affords a realistic challenge to the offensive team.

We normally try to teach pressing techniques during spring training, but if we feel that this time could be best utilized in teaching skills pertaining to some other area of the game, we alter the first two weeks of our after-school workout sessions to allow us the time to practice these drills.

DUMMY ASSIGNMENT DRILL

This drill is designed simply to teach the players the terminology and the principles of zone pressing, and their assignments. The defensive set of this drill initially is the 1-2-2 zone alignment (see Diagram 10-1). We call player #1 the "forcer." Her responsibility is to force the ball to the sideline. She will assume what we call an influence stance.

To teach this influence stance, we ask an offensive and defensive player to face one another about three feet apart. The offensive player is instructed to hold the ball in triple threat position on the right shoulder. The defensive player is told to place the wide-open palm of her right hand on the offensive player's left arm, shoulder high, as if she were actually giving her a gentle nudge in the direction she desires her to go. Her knees are bent, with the toes of the right foot pointing forward and the toes of the left foot pointing toward the sideline that she wishes to force her. Her left arm, with wide-open palm in the same plane as the ball, is extended and also pointing toward the designated sideline. The middle of the defensive player's body is in a direct line between the offensive player and the middle of the court, as penetration to the middle of the court would have the most damaging effect on the scheme of the press. Except for the actual contact of the defensive player's hand, this is the stance that the "forcer" is to maintain by shuffling, thus forcing the player with the ball to dribble to the sideline.

If the ball is forced toward her sideline, player #2 is called the "cutoff." Her responsibility is to cut off or stop any vertical dribbling

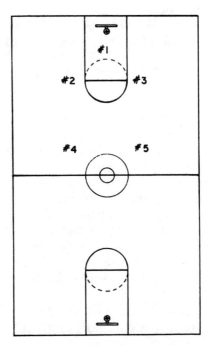

Diagram 10-1. Basic Set of Dummy Assignment Drill

action. She uses the same "heel-toe ball hawking" stance described in Chapter Four. The middle of her body is in a direct line between the offensive player and the opposite baseline. If the cutoff and forcer maintain their stances and fulfill their responsibilities of stopping middle and vertical penetration, they will form a trap along the sideline.

Once the trap is formed, player #3 assumes "middle" responsibility. This means that she is responsible for one of two things: either to stop the pass to the middle, or to arrive in time to assume a good heel-toe ball hawking stance to put pressure on the ball and stop vertical penetration, thus giving her teammates time to rotate to their new positions (see Diagram 10-2).

Player #4 assumes "sideline" responsibilities if the trap is formed along the sideline closest to her. She is also responsible for one of two things: either to stop the pass up the sideline, or to arrive in time to assume a good forcer or influence stance to stop penetration to the middle, thus giving her teammates time to rotate to their new positions (see Diagram 10-3).

If the trap is set along the sideline farthest from her, player #5 assumes "back" or safety responsibilities. She is the last line of defense between the opponents and their basket. She is responsible for one of three things: to stop the "bomb" or long pass; to arrive in time to assume a good forcer or influence stance to stop penetration to the mid-

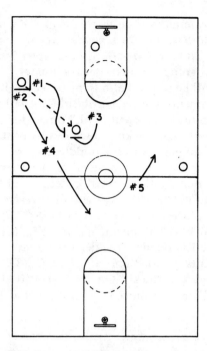

Diagram 10-2. Pass to Middle with Rotation of Positions

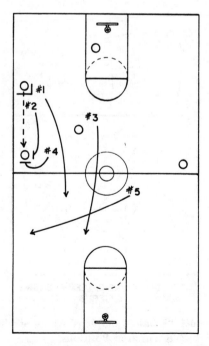

Diagram 10-3. Pass Along Sideline with Rotation of Positions

dle, thus giving teammates time to rotate to their new positions (see Diagram 10-4); or to retreat to the lane and prepare to follow the rules of defending a 2-on-1 situation (described in Chapter 1) if she sees that the offensive attack has gotten ahead of her teammates.

Should the ball be trapped along the other sideline, players #2 and #3 exchange assignments and responsibilities as will players #4 and #5. In the initial "Dummy Assignment Drill," three offensive players simply walk the ball down the court taking it from sideline, back to the middle, to the opposite sideline, back to the middle, etc. (see Diagram 10-5). As the ball is dribbled toward the right sideline, the defensive players shout out their assignments . . . #1, "Forcer!"; #2, "Cutoff!"; #3, "Middle!"; #4, "Sideline!"; and #5, "Back!" As the ball is reversed back out of the trap to O_1, all five of the defensive players holler, "Stay!" as they move back to their initial 1-2-2 alignment. When the ball is passed to O_3 who dribbles toward the left sideline, the defensive players once again shout out their assignments . . . #1, "Forcer!"; #3, "Cut-Off!"; #2, "Middle!"; #5, "Sideline!"; and #4, "Back!" On the reverse back to O_1, they once again holler "Stay!" as they move back to the initial 1-2-2 alignment.

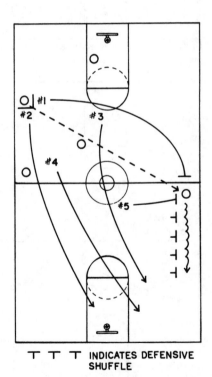

T T T INDICATES DEFENSIVE SHUFFLE

Diagram 10-4. "Bomb" Completed Along Sideline with Rotation of Positions

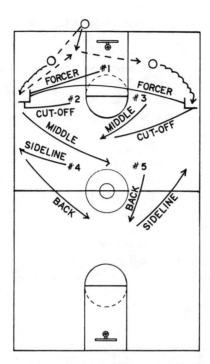

Diagram 10-5. Dummy Assignment Drill

This is a two-minute competitive drill. The blue team, X, plays defense first. Three red players, O, walk the ball down the floor as described above. The players shout out their responsibilities. Upon reaching the other end, the defensive players rotate positions, and the drill goes back down the floor, the other way this time. When the other end is reached, players rotate positions again.

We feel very strongly about every player on the team knowing every position. Should we have to resort to using a press, we do not have to worry about playing players according to their responsibilities on the press. Our philosophy of continuing our press after the first trap is broken often calls for players assuming new positions and responsibilities, thus we acquaint them with all positions in this dummy drill. Furthermore, we feel that by knowing the responsibilities of every position of a press, we can make better decisions in attacking it effectively.

After two minutes, the red team plays defense. Only negative points are tallied on the scoreboard clock. If the coach sees a miscue in execution or hears a player holler out the wrong player responsibility, he/she calls out "Point!" to the scorekeeper. At the end of the drill, the team with the greatest number of points has to run.

TWO-ON-ONE TRAPPING DRILL

In this drill, we practice the responsibilities of the forcer and the cutoff. The court is divided into four segments by placing chairs down the middle of it lengthwise (see Diagram 10-6). Two pair of red players play defense on one end and two pair of blue players play defense on the other. The offensive players, X_1 and X_2 and O_1 and O_2, each have a ball and try to dribble to the mid-court line against the two defenders in her segment of the court. The defenders, X_F and X_C and O_F and O_C, try to force a trap along the sideline or keep the player with the ball dribbling for five seconds closely guarded which results in a five-second violation, or they try to come up with a steal. Points are awarded as follows: a trap along the sideline is worth 3 points, a five-second violation is worth 2 points, and a steal is worth 1 point.

The offensive players rotate from line #1 to #2 and back to #1, etc. The defensive pairs play defense for two minutes, each changing forcer and cutoff responsibilities after each attempt to dribble up against them. At the end of two minutes, the defensive players go to offense and two pair of offensive players from each team come out to play defense. The

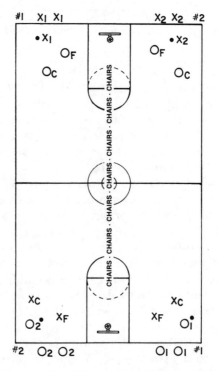

Diagram 10-6. Two-on-One Trapping Drill

drill continues until all players on the team have had the opportunity to play defense. Each defensive pair is responsible for shouting out their points to the scorekeeper. The players waiting in line are required to count, "One thousand and one, one thousand and two, etc." in order to determine the five-second violation. At the end of the drill, the losing team has to run.

THREE-ON-THREE TRAPPING DRILL

In this drill, three offensive players are trying to bring the ball up to mid-court against three defensive players (see Diagram 10-7). Let us say that the ball is passed in to player #2. She is to advance the ball up the sideline looking to pass to player #3 or #1. Player #3 is to go to the strongside corner, and player #1 is to flash up the middle of the court. It is the responsibility of the forcer and cutoff to play loose enough to assist the weakside cutoff, who now assumes middle responsibilities, to stop the pass to the cutters, thus forcing her to dribble. Once the ball is put on the floor, the forcer and cutoff go into action in an attempt to set

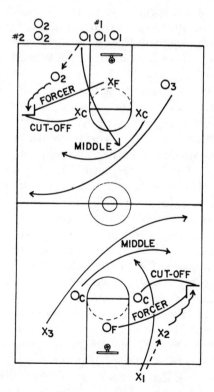

Diagram 10-7. Three-on-Three Trapping Drill

the trap along the sideline. Once the trap is set, the trapper's body should be at a 90-degree angle or form an "L." The cutoff's right foot and knee should be in contact with the forcer's left foot and knee. The defensive players should holler "Trap! Trap! Trap!" to signal the other players to get to their assigned positions. The trapper's hands should remain in the same plane as the ball making it difficult to pass, and at the same time, keeping players from reaching in and committing an unnecessary foul.

The weakside cutoff, who now assumes middle responsibilities, is introduced to "gapping." This means splitting the distance between two players or potentially dangerous areas of penetration by the pass. We instruct players to stop the "advancing up-court" pass to the middle first, as we feel that penetration by a pass or dribble to the middle of a containing zone press produces the greatest potential danger for our opponents to break the press effectively. In a containing zone, we allow the ball to be passed back out of the trap or even passed horizontally to the middle lane, as we feel that we have time to set up another trap with a minimal amount of ball advancement by the other team.

Thus, the middle player tries to position herself equidistant between player #3 in the corner and player #1 flashing to the middle. From this gapping position, she is ready to stop the pass or to arrive in time to assume cutoff responsibilities whether it be on a pass to the side-line or to the middle. (Refer back to the "middle" and "sideline" responsibilities of Diagrams 10-2 and 10-3.)

If the pass is reversed out of the trap backwards or horizontally to player #1, the defensive players holler "Stay!" and return to their original alignment. Player #3 is asked to return to the left side of the court to receive the ball and try her hand at advancing the ball up court. Player #2 goes to the left or strongside corner, and player #1 once again tries to flash up the middle. The same responsibilities for the right side of the court apply to the left side of the court except that the two cutoff players exchange middle and cutoff responsibilities. This "see-saw" action by the offensive players continues until they reach the mid-court line.

If the offense successfully reaches the mid-court line within ten seconds, no points are awarded. Should they fail to reach the mid-court line, but still be in possession of the ball within the ten-second time limit, the defensive team will receive two points. Should the defense force a turnover such as traveling, a bad pass, a charging foul, a five-second violation, etc., they are awarded two points. Should the defense come up with a steal, they should try to turn it into a basket. If they convert the steal into a basket, they are awarded two points. If they fail to score, however, they receive only one point.

If the pass is completed "up court" either to the player in the corner or the flasher up the middle, the defensive players holler "Bust!"

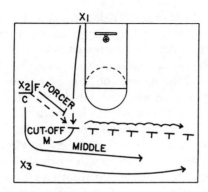

Diagram 10-8. Complete Pass over Trap to Middle "Flasher"

This signals prompt action and an exchange of responsibilities. If the pass is advanced up court to the flasher in the middle lane, the middle defender must arrive in time to act as a cutoff and stop vertical penetration. The forcer comes over to force the ball away from the middle, and the original cutoff now assumes middle responsibilities (see Diagram 10-8). Should the pass be completed to the sideline player, the defense once again hollers "Bust," and the middle defender must once again arrive in time to be the cutoff (see Diagram 10-9). This time, however, the original cutoff assumes forcer responsibilities in not allowing penetration to the middle, and the original forcer assumes the gapping responsibilities of the middle player.

Red plays defense on one end of the court while blue plays defense on the other. Each group of three stays on defense for three minutes, changing positions after each attempt by the offense to reach the mid-court line. Offensively, the players rotate from line #1 to #2 to #3 and back to #1, etc. At the end of three minutes, a new trio of defenders come

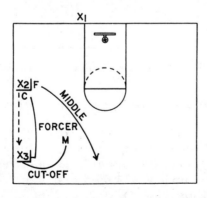

Diagram 10-9. Complete Pass over Trap to Sideline Player

out on the floor, and the original defenders take their place in the offensive lines. Play continues until all players have played defense.

The drill begins with the coach's whistle. This signals the ball to be passed in and the clock to start as soon as a player touches the ball. The clock will sound the buzzer and stop in ten-second intervals. The defenders change positions and ready themselves for another attack by three offensive players. This drill may be shortened to one or two minutes once the players feel comfortable in the mechanics of its execution. As always, the losing team will run at the end of the drill.

Later in the season, we will practice this drill out of a 2-1 denial alignment (see Diagram 10-10). When running a full-court press during a game, we almost always use a denial alignment. The reason for our teaching a 1-2-2 press that allows the first pass to be thrown in without any pressure is because we feel that its principles most easily conform to our odd-front three-quarter, half-court, or quarter-court presses that we occasionally employ—such as the 1-2-2, 1-2-1-1, or the 1-3-1.

Out of the denial alignment, the two players denying the ball are called forcers because if their player catches the ball, they are responsible for forcing them to the sideline. The back player is the cutoff for both forcers. The forcer whose player did not catch the ball assumes middle responsibilities. After the initial pass inbounds, the responsibilities are the same as for the 1-2 alignment, already discussed.

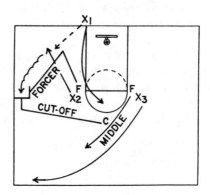

Diagram 10-10. Three-on-Three Drill out of a Denial Alignment

FOUR-ON-FOUR TRAPPING DRILL

This drill is similar to the three-on-three drill except that a fourth offensive and defensive player are added and the drill is played full-court (see Diagram 10-11). The blue team, X, is on defense first. The four defensive players line up in a 1-2-1 formation. If the ball is passed to O_2, O_4 looks for a sideline pass, O_3 flashes to the middle, and O_1 stays behind the ball for the reverse pass back out of the trap.

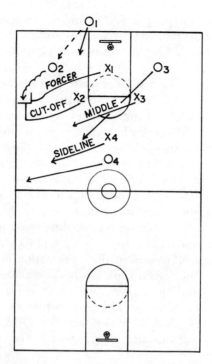

Diagram 10-11. Four-on-Four Trapping Drill

X_1 assumes the forcer role, and X_2 assumes cutoff responsibilities. Once again, they must play loose enough to assist their teammates in stopping the pass to the sideline or middle, thus forcing the dribble. X_3 moves to assume middle responsibilities, and X_4 assumes sideline responsibilities. It should be noted the X_3 and X_4 are instructed to gap—that is, position themselves equidistant from the two potentially dangerous areas they are defending (see Diagram 10-12). X_4 positions herself

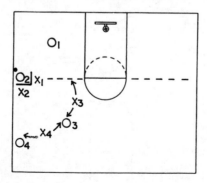

Diagram 10-12. "Gapping" Technique of Sideline and Middle Defenders

equidistant from the sideline player (O_4) and the middle player (O_3) and the horizontal plane of the ball. It is a containing zone, so according to our philosophy passes below the horizontal plane are not considered dangerous.

Once again, when the ball is reversed out of the trap to O_1, the defensive players shout out "Stay!" and quickly move to their original alignment. Player O_3 moves to the left side of the court to receive the pass from O_1, so that she can try her hand at advancing the ball up the floor. O_4 moves to the strongside sideline and O_2 flashes to the middle, while O_1 continues to position herself behind the ball looking for the reverse out of the trap. The defensive assignments would be the same as they were on the opposite side of the floor, except that X_3 would become the cutoff and X_2 would assume middle responsibilities. X_1 would remain the forcer and X_4 would resume sideline responsibilities.

In case of a completed pass to the middle player, X_3 must arrive in time to serve as the cutoff to stop further penetration of the middle. The pass over the trap is once again signaled by the defensive players shouting "Bust," thus signaling a possible change in responsibilities. X_1 remains the forcer, X_2 assumes middle responsibilities, and X_4 continues to shoulder sideline responsibilities (see Diagram 10-13). Should the pass be completed to the sideline player, X_4 must arrive in time to be the

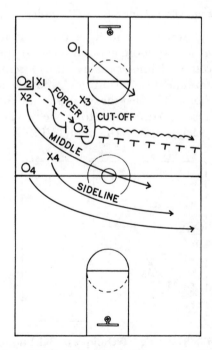

Diagram 10-13. Pass over the Trap to the Middle

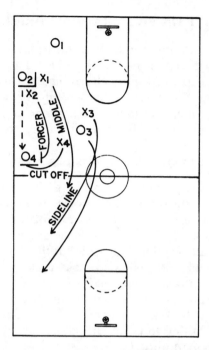

Diagram 10-14. Pass over the Trap to the Sideline

cutoff; X_2 slides down to become the forcer; X_3 assumes sideline responsibilities; and X_1 assumes middle responsibilities (see Diagram 10-14).

So far, we have only discussed ball advancement by passing over the trap. The ball could, however, be advanced up court by dribbling up the sideline after a defensive miscue by the cutoff and forcer defenders. Regardless of how the ball is advanced to these areas, the coverage remains the same, with the middle defender assuming cutoff responsibilities if the ball penetrates to the middle and the sideline defender assuming cutoff responsibilities if the penetration is up the sideline.

This drill is a three-minute drill with both the offense and defense trying to score points. Each time the offensive team scores a basket, it receives two points. It also scores two points whenever it penetrates past the free throw line. If the offense sees no sure-fire scoring opportunity, the players holler "Set up!" and go into a 1-4 offensive alignment. We never encourage forcing a shot in any of our drills.

The defensive players change positions each trip down the floor. They score points in the same manner as described for the three-on-three drill. The clock, however, will not sound a ten-second count, so it is up to the coach to officiate the drill as if it were a game. After three minutes, the teams change from offense to defense. At the end of the drill—each team having played offense and defense for three minutes—the losing team has to run.

FIVE-ON-FIVE TRAPPING DRILL

Following the four-on-four drill, the only player responsibility left to add to the press is that of the "back" player. The responsibilities of this position were explained quite clearly in the Dummy Assignment Drill except, perhaps, for the rules that govern whether the back player should: 1. stop the "bomb" or long pass, 2. arrive in time to assume the forcer role, or 3. retreat to the lane preparing to defend a 2-on-1 situation.

The rules to be followed by the back player are as follows:

1. A long pass out of a trapping situation should be "open game" to the players down court, as the ball will most likely be in the air a long time because of the arch and the distance it must travel. If you have the angle and ability to make a clean interception, "go for it." If there is any doubt in your mind as to your ability to make a clean interception, then be content to execute properly one of the two remaining options. You are the last line of defense between the opponents and their basket, so a poor decision in attempting to intercept and failing to do so will almost always lead to an easy scoring opportunity.

2. If the pass is completed to the middle area of the court that the back player is responsible for, retreat to the lane and prepare to defend a 2-on-1 situation. A pass to the deep middle of the court is too dangerous to defend, with the possibility of setting up another trapping situation. Due to the gapping alignment of the middle and sideline defenders in respect to the offensive players in their areas, the defenders would most likely lose a foot race down the court, as the opponents would have a three- to six-foot lead on them in down-court position. A quick pass from the middle receiver to the players cutting to the basket would result in an easy two points (see Diagram 10-15).

3. If the ball is passed deep to the sideline, the back player may assume a forcer stance if she feels that she has the ability to put enough pressure on the ball to cause a poor pass to a player cutting to the basket, or if she feels she can force the opponent to put the ball on the floor and then contain her along the sideline with the intent of trapping her in the corner. (Refer back to Diagram 10-4.) This calls for good athletic ability or good decision making in judging your ability in comparison to the player receiving the pass. If you feel that you are outclassed, retreat to the lane and prepare to play 2-on-1 defense. Once again, confidence in pressuring and con-

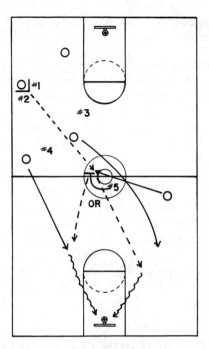

Diagram 10-15. Avoid Trapping Long Pass to Middle

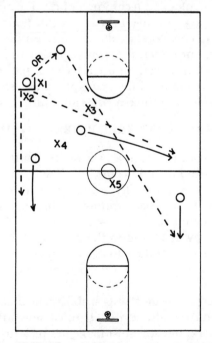

Diagram 10-16. Five-on-Five Long Pass Drill Options

taining the opponent is admirable, but a foolhardy decision will be disastrous to the team.

With these rules in mind, a three-minute 5-on-5 drill is ready to begin. The blue team, X, is on defense only for the first three-minute period. All players will practice all positions. The red team, O, is on offense and will try to score specifically using the long pass. It can be thrown over the trap or by player, O_1, on the reverse out of the trap (see Diagram 10-16). To keep the front players honest, two points are awarded the offensive team each time they cross the mid-court line using the dribble; two points are also awarded the offensive team each time they complete a long pass. Two additional points are awarded if a basket is scored following the dribbling penetration of the mid-court line or the completion of a bomb. Two points are also awarded if the players upon penetrating below the free throw line recognize that no easy scoring opportunity is available, and holler "Set up" and go into a 1-4 offensive alignment. Defensively, points are scored in the same manner as described in the three-on-three drill. After three minutes, the teams change from offense to defense with the losing team having to run after this final three-minute period.

RUN AND JUMP PRESS DRILLS

Once the principles and techniques of a full-court press have been taught, it is quite easy to convert them to a three-quarter, half-court or quarter-court press. Therefore, we do not work on these particular types of presses in drills, but rather, in scrimmage situations. In teaching the run and jump press, however, we use a series of half-court break-down drills. Once we have mastered the principles and techniques of the run and jump, we expand it to three-quarter and full-court play.

THREE-ON-THREE PINBALL GAME

This drill is confined to the area of the court between the hash marks or time lines and the mid-court line. Two minutes are put on the clock. The blue team, X, is on offense and the red team, O, is on defense. The game begins with the coach rolling the ball to either X_1 or X_3 (see Diagram 10-17). These two players are the scorers. The only way they can score points is by dribbling to the hash mark on their end of the court and touching it with their foot. Each time they accomplish this, one point is tallied on the scoreboard clock, and the coach rolls the ball in once again.

It is the defensive team's responsibility to practice the run and jump techniques during this drill. O_1 must not only stop the drive toward the hash mark, but she must make her pick up the ball. She can best accomplish this by using a heel-toe stance and a sweeping action with the right hand, while she literally tries to put her head on the ball.

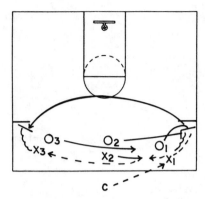

Diagram 10-17. Three-on-Three Run and Jump Drill

The sweeping action—right arm extended, palm wide open facing the ball, and not more than four inches off the floor—prevents a crossover dribble, while the motion of a defender's head coming right toward the ball will force a reverse or cause the player to pick the ball up. As soon as O_2 sees X_1's back turned toward her, she begins to cheat toward her. As X_1 attempts the reverse, O_2 seals the trap causing her to pick up the ball.

In the meantime, O_3 has begun to cheat toward X_2, who is referred to as the "flipper," because she can only pass the ball to the other side of the court than from where she received it. O_3 may try for the interception, but if she chooses not to, she arrives as X_2 receives the ball and puts as much pressure as possible on the flipper to delay the pass or cause it to be thrown poorly.

As soon as the ball is picked up by X_1, O_1 circles away from the trap and heads to the other side of the court to either intercept the pass or to stop X_3's attempt to dribble to the hash mark on that side of the floor. O_3 now cheats over to seal the trap on X_3, and O_2 cheats over to defend the flipper.

The drill continues for two minutes with all players changing positions on offense and defense. After each score, interception, or violation, the ball is passed out to the coach who once again rolls it in to begin play. At the end of two minutes, two new trios step in to practice the drill. After all of the red players have played defense, blue goes on defense. At the end of the drill, the losing team has to run.

FOUR-ON-FOUR PINBALL GAME

We now add a fourth player to the drill. This player is also a scorer. She is restricted to playing only in the top half of the jump ball circle. She can only score points by touching the free throw line with her foot and is allowed only one dribble (see Diagram 10-18).

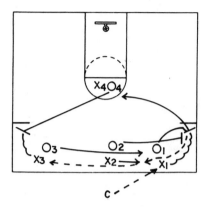

Diagram 10-18. Four-on-Four Run and Jump Drill

The three players above the time-line marks follow the same rules as before. O_4, however, is now involved in the rotation. As soon as X_1 picks up the ball, O_1 circles away from the trap and "bumps off" (relieves her of her responsibility), O_4. O_4 is now responsible for an interception or stopping X_3's attempt to dribble to the hash mark.

With the ball on this side of the court, O_3 now cheats over to seal the trap on X_3, and O_2 cheats over to defend the "flipper." As soon as the ball is picked up, O_4 heads toward the free throw line scorer and bumps off O_1, who must hustle to defend X_1 once again.

It should be noted that the three players above the time line may pass the ball to the free throw line scorer at any time. If her attempt to score at the free throw line is stopped, she may pass the ball back out to either of the three players to continue play. Scoring, rotation, and running stipulations remain the same as described for the three-on-three drill.

FIVE-ON-FIVE PINBALL GAME

For this drill, a fifth player is added. This player is also a scorer. She may score one point either by stepping on the square on both sides of the free throw line or by actually scoring a basket. She is limited to three dribbles and to moving along the baseline only. She is instructed to stay even with the ball (see Diagram 10-19).

There are now five players involved in the rotation. As soon as X_1 picks up the ball, O_1 circles away from the trap and bumps off O_5, who moves to the free throw area and bumps off O_4, who must once again hustle to defend X_3.

With the ball being on this side of the court, O_3 cheats over to seal the trap; O_2 cheats off to defend the flipper. As soon as the ball is picked

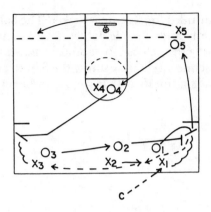

Diagram 10-19. Five-on-Five Run and Jump Drill

up by X_3, O_4 circles away from the trap and bumps off O_1, who in turn bumps off O_5, who must now hustle to defend X_1 (see Diagram 10-20).

Scoring, rotation, and running stipulations remain the same as described for the other drills until the players feel confident in their job responsibilities. Once they have mastered the drill, do not make them throw the ball out to the coach after scoring by touching the hash marks, free throw line, or squares. Just have the coach holler out "Point" each time they score in this manner. The game will take on a much quicker playing action and the coach will find himself/herself shouting "Point! Point! Point! etc.," over and over again until the scene truly takes on the resemblance of a giant-sized pinball game.

The game would differ in that three minutes would be put on the clock, with it stopping and starting as it would in a game situation. One point would be awarded for touching the lines or the squares, and two

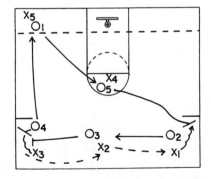

Diagram 10-20. Five-on-Five Run and Jump Drill (Continued)

points would be awarded for scoring a basket. The ball would be thrown out to the coach only after a made basket, a violation by the offense, or possession gained by the defense. It should be noted that the free throw line scorer and baseline scorer may throw the ball to any one of the other four players. This is a fun drill that we use to bring a boring workout session to life.

11

Attacking the Press More Effectively

Initial observation of the press breaker that we employ may lead one to believe that it is unorthodox. An in-depth analysis of our method of breaking the press, however, will reveal some very sound principles of basketball. In developing our press breaker philosophy, we established the following rules:

1. Never throw the ball over a trap. Always look to reverse the ball instead. If the reverse pass is denied, step through the trap, pass under or around the trap, but never over it.

2. Attack the press; do not be satisfied with merely breaking it. Look at presses as "golden opportunities" for scoring quickly and surely.

3. Breaking a press is a team effort. Every player must be well-versed in the responsibilities of every position.

In our last five appearances at the state tournament, we have faced South Oak Cliff of Dallas four times in the championship game and Jack Yates of Houston in two semi-final and one final game. Each year, therefore, we assume that in order to win the State Championship, we will, in all probability, have to defeat a very talented South Oak Cliff or Jack Yates team whose formidable successes can largely be attributed to tenacious full-court and half-court presses. They trap with very tall personnel whose jumping ability and quickness would make many boys' teams envious.

Experience has taught us one lesson: We cannot beat these teams' presses by any attempts to throw over their traps. We have, therefore, developed a style of press breaker that features ball reversal.

THE PHILOSOPHY OF BALL REVERSAL

Our method of breaking the press appears unorthodox because, contrary to most coaching strategies, we initiate our attack by having the player receiving the inbound pass turn and dribble up the sideline until the opponents come up and set a trap. This makes the opposing team think we are falling right into their press plan. Once we have made them form a trap on or near the sideline, coverage of the entire floor, except for the small area where the trap has been set, becomes the responsibility of three defensive players. With rare exception, most presses that form a sideline trap have one player designated to cover the sideline area; another player is delegated the responsibility of stopping all passes to the middle of the court. The remaining player is usually responsible for covering the back of the press, or in other words, the long pass (see Diagram 11-1).

Once we have made the press shift to these designated areas, we feel that we have the edge on our opponents because we know the location of every defensive player on the court. This not only makes them more susceptible to our offensive plan of action, but it simplifies our having to make constant adjustments to the many types of presses that can be employed—1-2-2 presses, 1-3-1 presses, 2-2-1 presses, etc.

Entire books have been written on breaking the press. It is impossible to attack every press differently. Such tactics, in my estimation, would make the players feel unprepared and lacking in confidence whenever a new formation would be encountered. In the waning moments of a big game, a team's lack of confidence could make the difference between winning and losing. Therefore, regardless of the press formation, we always have one plan of action in which the players are well-versed.

In the ideal game situation, we like to have our play-maker, desig-

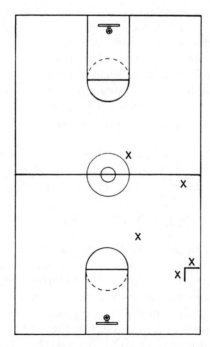

Diagram 11-1. Press Assignments of Floor Coverage After Sideline Trap Has Been Set

nated as player #1, throw the ball in from under the basket (see Diagram 11-2). Many coaches prefer using a tall post player at this position, reasoning that in case the defending team chooses to put pressure on the inbounds pass, a tall player would have a better chance of not having their view obstructed. I, however, feel that it takes the most poised player on the team, who is usually the play-maker, to make the right decision in getting the ball inbounds. First of all, at no other point during the press will the ball be closer to the opposing team's basket than on the inbounds pass, and secondly, while the ball is being thrown in, the defense actually has an on-the-court advantage of five against four. They can capitalize on this advantage in many ways. For example, they may choose to double-team our favorite inbounds receiver; they may invite us to throw long; or they may align themselves in such a way as to influence our inbounds pass to a particular area of the floor. Therefore, I feel, that the first pass into the court is actually the most critical in consistently attacking the press.

We fill the #2 and #3 spots with forward-type players who are adept at getting open for the inbounds pass. They, too, must exhibit a high degree of poise, as they must initiate our attack by dribbling up the sideline inviting a trap. Once the trap is set, they must retain composure

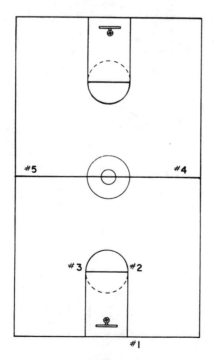

Diagram 11-2. Initial Set of Press Breaker

in quickly reversing the ball out of the trap to player #1 who has stepped inbounds and positioned herself in an area lower than the trap (see Diagram 11-3). Once the player dribbling into the trap has passed off the ball, she takes off down the sideline toward her goal.

While player #2 is initiating the dribble up the sideline, player #5 (a position we like to fill with our best ball-handling post player) moves toward player #4 and sets a screen on the defensive player who has the responsibility of stopping the sideline pass. Using a reverse pivot, she quickly opens up toward the ball attempting to split the defense by positioning herself halfway between the defender, who has sideline responsibility, and the player assigned the responsibility of stopping the pass to the middle. This screen and roll action by player #5 is extremely important to the success of our press breaker, because it not only makes the defense think that we are further falling into their press plans by having four players positioned on one side of the court, but it also causes confusion as to who is to cover player #5 once she has positioned herself between the sideline and middle defender.

Player #4, a position we try to fill with a post player, fakes down toward the trapped player setting up the sideline defender for the screen. She then reels off the screen looking over her shoulder and heads toward

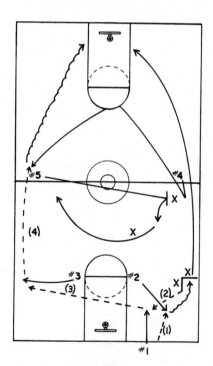

Diagram 11-3. Full Court Press Breaker with "Sideline" Option

our goal in the mid-area of the court. Once she reaches the top of the circle, she cuts sharply toward the opposite sideline looking for the pass from player #3.

Reversal Denial Options

Our first option is to reverse the ball from player #2 to player #1 to player #3, who has positioned herself in an area along the opposite sideline, even with or lower than the initial trap. On receiving the ball, player #3 looks toward the middle faking a pass to player #5 who has continued to move in a circular pattern even with the ball in the middle of the floor. She then fires the ball to player #4 who is coming toward the ball along the sideline. We call this our "sideline" option. Upon receiving the ball, player #4 *drives hard* for the basket hoping to capitalize on a 2-on-1 situation against the back defender with the help of player #2 who has been moving up the opposite sideline.

Our second option is to pass the ball from player #1 or player #3 to player #5 who has been asking for the ball in the middle of the court. We call this our "middle" option. Upon receiving the ball, player #5 drives hard down the middle of the court hoping to capitalize on a 3-on-2 situation with player #4 and player #2 who have filled the side lanes (see Diagram 11-4).

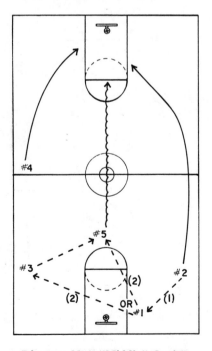

Diagram 11-4. "Middle" Option

If players #4 and #5 are not open, our third option is to have player #3 drive hard diagonally toward the middle of the court hoping to capitalize on a 3-on-2 situation with players #4 and #2. Player #5 becomes the trailer. We call this our "dribble" option (see Diagram 11-5).

When the defense begins to overreact to the ball reversal action, we use our fourth option. In this option, player #1 sees that the defense is leaving their strongside press assignments too quickly to cover player #2 who is sprinting up the sideline. Player #1 fakes the reverse to player #3, then quickly fires the ball back to player #2. On receiving the pass, she drives hard toward the basket looking to capitalize on a 2-on-1 situation with player #4. We call this our "fake reverse" option (see Diagram 11-6).

It should be noted that in all of these options, our plan of attack involved ball reversal out of the trap. But what if the reverse pass is denied? There are generally two ways in which the reverse is denied. First of all, the horizontal trapper will move to deny the pass out of the trap (see Diagram 11-7). This produces a gap between the two trappers. Since our players are instructed to use a reverse pivot to throw the ball out of the trap, the pivot foot will be that foot which is closest to the trappers. As player #2 starts the reverse pivot only to have it denied, she uses the crossover technique to step around and bring the ball over the head of the vertical trapper. Seeing that the reverse pass is being denied, signals player #1 to cut. A quick chest pass to #1 keys the middle player

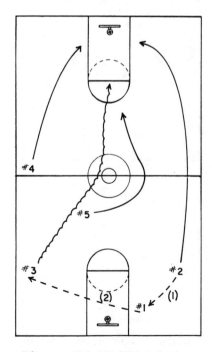

Diagram 11-5. "Dribble" Option

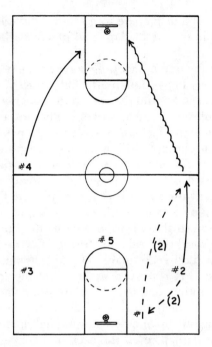

Diagram 11-6. "Fake Reverse" Option

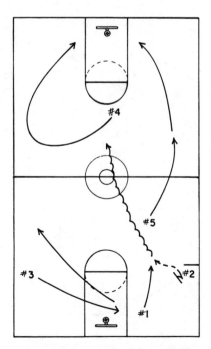

Diagram 11-7. "Cutter" Option

to take the side lane and prepare to go down the floor 3-on-2, with #1 handling the ball in the middle lane and player #4 filling the other side lane.

Having split the trap by stepping between the two defenders, player #2 needs to have her elbows out and the ball under her chin to protect it as she prepares to pass. Should the pass to the cutter, #1, be denied by the middle defender, player #5 cuts right behind her toward the ball looking for the pass (see Diagram 11-8). If she receives the pass, she takes the ball to the middle, with player #1 filling the right lane and player #4 filling the left lane. Player #5 may even be able to pass the ball to #1 for a 2-on-1 situation with player #4. If neither of these passes can be completed, player #2 may use a reverse crossover pivot to throw the ball back out of the trap to player #3 who fills #1's vacant spot. The press breaker is now run as described above for the reverse out of the trap, except that #4 moves to the weakside sideline filling #3's vacated spot and #1 assumes the responsibilities of player #4 (see Diagram 11-9).

We call these three reversal denial options the "cutter" option, the "cross the cutter" option, and the "filler" option. These options will be just as effective if the method of denying the reverse pass is not by the horizontal trapper, but by another player such as the middle defender cheating down, or perhaps even the back or sideline defender cheating down (see Diagram 11-10).

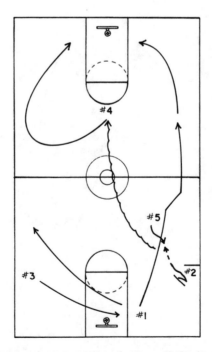

Diagram 11-8. "Cross the Cutter" Option

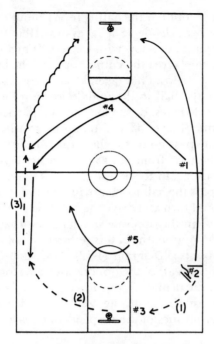

Diagram 11-9. "Filler" Option

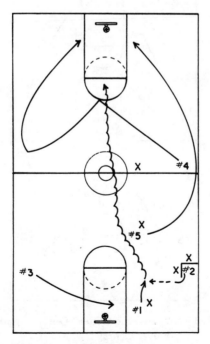

Diagram 11-10. "Cutter" Option Against Third Player Denial

On the "cutter" option, the ball is reversed out of the trap to #1 as she cuts to get past her defender. She takes the ball to the middle looking for a 3-on-2 situation to develop with players #4 and #5 who are filling the side lanes. On the "cross the cutter" option, the ball is reversed out of the trap to #5 as she loses her defender by crossing behind #1 on the cut. She may drive the ball to the middle looking for a 3-on-2 with #1 and #4 filling the side lanes, or she may choose to pass the ball to #3 on the opposite sideline. Player #3 was planning to fill #1's vacated spot, but upon seeing the pass go to #5, she returns to her original position. Upon receiving the pass from #5, #3 may either drive the ball to the middle looking once again for a 3-on-2 with #4 and #1 filling the side lanes, or she may pass the ball to #4 moving toward it near the mid-court area. Player #4 would turn and drive the ball toward the basket trying to score 2-on-1 with #1 in the opposite side lane (see Diagram 11-11).

On the "filler" option, the ball is reversed out of the trap to #3 who fills #1's vacated spot (see Diagram 11-12). As described before, the press breaker is now run with all of the options available for our regular press breaker play without denial of the reverse pass, except that #4 now assumes the responsibilities of the weakside sideline player and #1 assumes the responsibilities of the deep sideline player.

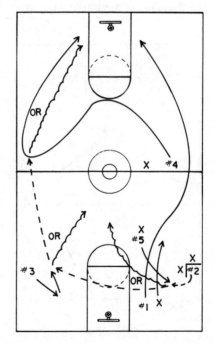

Diagram 11-11. "Cross the Cutter" Option Against Third Player Denial

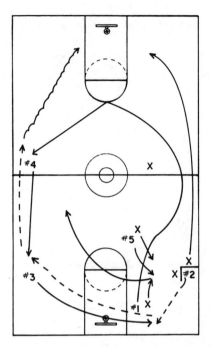

Diagram 11-12. "Filler" Option Against Third Player Denial

It should be noted that in all of these options, our plan of attack is to *drive hard* to set up a scoring opportunity. We are not merely satisfied in getting the ball across the mid-court line within the ten-second time limit. If we merely breathe a sigh of relief for having beaten the ten-second count, we will probably find ourselves being pressed the entire game. If our plan of attack, however, is consistently successful in producing points for us, we will soon find our opponents pulling out of their press. We will then have the luxury of bringing the ball up court unharassed.

Should none of these options develop, we merely continue the same attack from the other side of the court (see Diagram 11-13). Player #3 dribbles up the sideline inviting the trap. Once the trap is set, she quickly reverses the ball to player #1 and heads toward our goal up the sideline. Upon seeing that nothing has developed, player #2 retreats back down the opposite sideline preparing to receive the reverse pass from player #1. Player #5 once again screens the sideline defensive player; #4 once again heads toward our basket and then sharply V's toward the ball on the opposite sideline. We refer to this as a "seesaw" option.

The final consideration that we must take into account in developing our press breaker is the fact that although we would prefer that our players man certain positions of the press breaker, we must be prepared

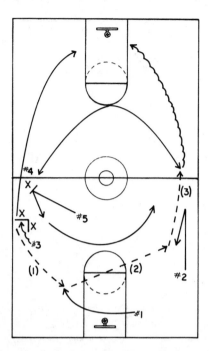

Diagram 11-13. "See-Saw" Option

for situations to arise where our personnel will be required to perform successfully at different assignments. For this reason, we insist that every player know the responsibilities of every position in the press breaker. This eliminates problems associated with substitutions. In critical situations, I am free to make substitutions without having to worry about the different combinations affecting my team's ability to break the press.

For example, with 10 seconds left on the clock, the score may be tied with our opponents going to the line for a fouled-on-the-shot free throw. I call my last timeout to discuss team strategy. The opposing team has a definite height advantage of three inches at the forward position. I need to make certain that we get the rebound should the shot be missed. Also, I need to substitute the forward position with one of my post players to take away the height advantage. Should the free throw be made, giving our opponents a one point lead, I would also have to instruct one of my post players to grab the ball out of the net to make the inbounds pass, as it would take too much time for our play-maker to come from her safety position of our free throw alignment to initiate the break.

If every player on the team did not know the responsibilities of every position on the press breaker, I would be fearful that this particular substitution and change of inbounding the ball assignment may dampen our effort in getting the ball down the court against the opponent's very aggressive press in time to score. I would be forced to gamble in making these strategic decisions. However, since my teams have been taught the responsibilities of every position in the press breaker, I simply make these adjustments with the confidence of knowing that I have negated the opponent's height advantage and that even should they take the lead, we will, in all probability, have the composure to attack their press effectively and have enough time to set up a scoring opportunity.

DUMMY PRESS BREAKER DRILL
WITH EIGHT OPTIONS

The first drill that we use in teaching the press breaker is called the "Dummy Press Breaker" drill. The purpose of this drill is to teach every player on our team the assignments of every position in our press breaker. We do this drill without any defensive players, thus giving it the name of "dummy drill." We are looking for the proper execution of the assigned responsibilities of each position.

Points of proper execution for each of the positions would be as follows:

Player #1:

1. Position yourself to the side of the backboard—not behind it—so that it will not interfere in passing the ball in.

2. Put both hands on the ball to avoid the temptation of throwing a long pass, which is more likely to be intercepted than the short, crisp passes that we prefer to use in attacking the press.

3. Wait until your teammates have quickly positioned themselves to start the break.

4. Slap the ball as a signal for players #2 and #3 to make their break in getting open for the inbounds pass.

5. Step off the baseline 2 feet to 3 feet if you are being pressured. Fake a pass or two to keep the defender off balance.

6. *Do not run* along the baseline. It is difficult enough to pass the ball to a moving target without your moving too.

7. Do not panic and try to force the pass in. It is the responsibility of your teammates to get open. We would rather give up the ball on a five-second count and have the opportunity of setting up our defense than to throw a pass that might be intercepted and turned into an easy bucket for our opponents.

8. Once you have passed the ball in, step onto the court staying

lower than the ball. Position yourself and move as necessary to safely receive the ball on the pass back out of the trap. Use the cutter option when the reverse out of the trap is being denied.

9. Upon receiving the ball, read the defense. Pass the ball using short, crisp passes. We are not looking for the bomb.

10. Stay lower than the ball acting as a safety for throwing the ball to you out of any traps that may form. This is also important, as you will be the sole defender between them and the basket should an interception occur.

11. Act as a leader in shouting commands to your teammates. You are in the most advantageous position on the court to read the defense.
   a. Should an interception occur, bide for time using defensive fakes. Do not under any circumstances give them an "uncalled for" three-point play.

Players #2 and #3:

1. Quickly take your position at the free throw line to start the break. Use screen and roll action to get yourself open should there be heavy denial on the inbounds pass. Meet the pass.

2. Upon receiving the inbounds pass, turn up court to face the defense.

3. If you are not trapped immediately, initiate a dribble up the sideline. Keep dribbling up the sideline until you are trapped, unless you have reached the time-line before the mid-court line. From this point, initiate a diagonal dribble. This signals a "stack" set for the half-court or three-quarter-court press breaker. Do not cross the mid-court line or pick up the ball until you know where you are going to pass it. (The "stack" set will be discussed later in this chapter.)

4. Should you be trapped before the time-line, pick up the ball as the trap forms and attempt to use a reverse pivot to protect the ball as you look over your shoulder to see if player #1 is open for the return pass.

5. Do not panic if player #1 is not immediately open for the return pass. Keep your back to one of the defenders in the trap and attempt to bring the ball over the other defender's head and step through the gap in the trap if there is one. If there is no gap, keep moving the ball in an up and down motion to keep the other defender from tying it up.

6. Do not force the pass. It is the responsibility of your team-mates to get open. Once again, we would rather give up the ball on a five-second count than give the opponents an easy bucket.

7. Once you have made the reverse pass back out of the trap, sprint down the sideline toward our goal. You must be under our bucket in time to capitalize on the 2-on-1 or 3-on-2 situation that develops. If you had to step through the trap to deliver the pass on the cutter or cross the cutter option, be prepared to fill a lane as the trailer or assume safety responsibilities if you are the last man down court.

8. Look over your shoulder as you sprint down the sideline giving a target for a return pass from player #1 should the "fake reverse" option develop. Be prepared to retreat quickly should we have to resort to our seesaw option.

9. If you are the player at the #2 or #3 position without the ball, quickly position yourself along the sideline opposite the ball. Remember to stay even or lower than the trap and move as necessary to receive the pass from #1. Also, be ready to fill #1's vacated spot should there be denial on the reverse pass forcing her to cut.

10. Do not try to force the pass to #4 or #5 on the "dribble" option. Once again, we would rather lose the ball on a ten-second violation than give the opponents the ball on an interception or forced dribble. Do not panic and rush the seesaw option.

   a. Should an interception occur, immediately retreat to the middle of the lane to assist #1 on defense.

Player #4:

1. Quickly take your position ball side one step above the mid-court line to start the break.

2. As the ball is being advanced up the sideline into the trap, fake down toward the ball to set up the sideline defender for the screen and roll action of #5.

3. As soon as the screen is set, reel off of the screen and head toward our goal up the middle of the court. Look over your shoulder and give a target for the pass to keep the back defender honest.

4. Upon reaching the top of the circle, cut sharply toward the opposite sideline looking for the pass from #3. Move as neces-

sary in your assigned area of the court to receive the pass. Meet the pass.

5. Upon receiving the pass, turn up court to face the defense, then drive hard toward our goal to set up a 2-on-1 situation.

6. Do not force the break. Should the 2-on-1 situation not develop, hold the ball and prepare to set up our regular offensive pattern.

7. Should the middle or dribble option develop, sprint toward the basket in your lane to set up a 3-on-2 situation.

8. Should the fake reverse option develop, fill the lane opposite the ball to set up a 2-on-1 situation.

9. Should the seesaw option develop, repeat your same assignment except that this time it will be on the opposite side of the floor.

10. Should the cutter options develop, be ready to fill your lane for the 3-on-2 or to receive a pass for a 2-on-1 situation.

11. Should the filler option develop, be ready to hustle up court to assume the responsibilities of the weakside sideline player.

12. Should the break be initiated (ball dribbled into the trap) on the opposite side of the floor, your responsibilities would become that of player #5 (see Diagram 11-14).
    a. Should the ball be intercepted, retreat quickly to set up our defense.

Player #5:

1. Quickly take your position weakside on step above the midcourt line to start the break.

2. Should #2 and #3 have trouble getting open for the inbounds pass, break toward the ball down the middle of the court.

3. As the ball is being advanced up the sideline into the trap, run toward player #4 and set a screen on the sideline defender.

4. Reverse immediately upon setting the screen and open up toward the ball. Slide to a position halfway between the sideline and middle defender.

5. Stay low and wide and put both hands up toward the ball making a "big" target in the middle of the floor.

6. As the ball is reversed, use a sliding motion to continue in a circular pattern staying even with the ball in the middle of the court.

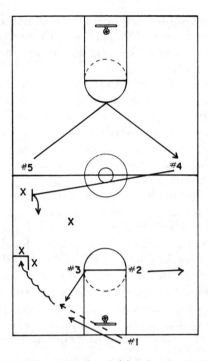

Diagram 11-14. Press Breaker Initiated to Left Side of Floor

7. Upon receiving the ball, turn up court to face the defense. *Drive hard* down the middle of the court to set up a 3-on-2 situation.

8. Should the dribble or cutter option develop, clear the middle for the dribbler and then follow up the attack as a trailer on the dribble option and side lane player on the cutter option.

9. Should the seesaw option develop, repeat your same assignment except that this time it will be on the opposite side of the floor.

10. Should the cross the cutter option develop, be sure to cross right behind player #1 using her as a screen to rid yourself of your defender. Upon receiving the ball, be sure to look up court before initiating your dribble as a pass to #3 may be wide open, thus moving the ball up court much faster.

11. Should the break be initiated on your side of the floor, your responsibilities would become that of player #4 (see Diagram 11-14).
    a. Should the ball be intercepted, retreat quickly to set up our defense.

The players will form lines in the area of our initial set for the press breaker (see Diagram 11-15). They will rotate from line to line of position #1 to #2 to #3, etc. They are to execute the above-described assignments of each position properly.

Three minutes are put on the clock. The drill begins on a signal from the coach. The coach, standing under the basket, shouts out two instructions as the first five players take their positions on the court. The first instruction—"right or left"—tells #1 whether to inbound the pass to the player on the right or left, so that the press breaker may be practiced from both sides. The second instruction—"middle," "sideline," "dribble," etc.—tells the group which option to run.

This drill may be made competitive in several ways. The coach may present the team with a challenge. For example, "Every time I see an error in execution I will holler out the word 'point' to the score-keeper. She will put one point on the scoreboard for the miscue in execution. If you have over 10 points at the end of the three minutes, the entire team will have to run a 'horse.'" (Or, the coach may issue the threat of one sprint for every point over 10.) The coach may also make the following stipulation: "To make this more interesting, the group of five players on the court at the time of a miscue, will have to run a lap before rotating to their next position. And don't be loafing on the lap! If

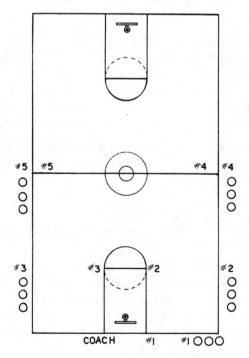

Diagram 11-15. Dummy Press Breaker Drill

anyone misses her turn, the entire team will have to run an additional horse at the end of the drill." (The coach may choose to lower the 10-point challenge to 9, 8, etc., as the season progresses. He/she may also wish to offer the reward of a water break, ending practice five minutes early, etc., for a perfect score of 0.)

The drill could be made competitive in another way by having another team on an adjacent court do the same drill. The team with the lowest score would win. The losing team would have to run.

TWO-ON-ONE PRESS BREAKER DRILL

The next drill that we use in teaching the press breaker is called the "2-on-1 Press Breaker." The purpose of this drill is to review the assignments of every position further and to develop our 2-on-1 attack of the "sideline" option, "fake reverse" option, "filler" option, or a sideline attack of the "cross the cutter" option.

There will be two teams on one court this time. X will be the red team and O will be the blue team. They will once again position themselves in the area of our initial set of the press breaker, and rotation will be the same as in the Dummy Press Breaker. This time, however, the player in position #1 of the team without the ball must step out and play defense against the offensive attack of the "sideline," "fake reverse," "filler," or "cross the cutter" options of the press breaker. The group of five who had just finished playing offense step off the court and rotate to their next position (see Diagram 11-16).

Four minutes are put on the clock. The coach, standing in the middle of the court, once again shouts two instructions—right or left and "sideline," "fake reverse," "filler," or "cross the cutter sideline." This signals which side the ball should be passed inbounds and what option of the press breaker should be executed.

The scoring is as follows: "Every time I holler out 'point' for an error in execution, one point will be put on the scoreboard clock for the *defending* team. You will get two points per basket on offense. Now remember, this time your points for miscues of execution will be given to the other team. The team with the highest score at the end of the drill wins. The losers will have to run a horse. Furthermore, the players will have to follow the rules for a 2-on-1 situation. (Refer to Chapter Three for rules.)

THREE-ON-TWO PRESS BREAKER DRILL

The next drill that we use in furthering our attacking phase of the press breaker is the "3-on-2 Press Breaker." The rules of the game and scoring are the same as those described for the "2-on-1 Press Breaker." The rotation is the same except that this time the #2 and #3 positions

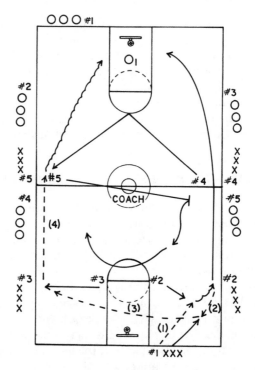

Diagram 11-16. "Two-on-One Press Breaker"

align themselves in a tandem to play defense in the 3-on-2 situation that will develop from our "middle," "dribble," "cutter," "cross the cutter," or "filler" options (see Diagram 11-17). The coach will once again shout out the direction to initiate the attack and what option to execute. Furthermore, the players will have to follow the rules for a 3-on-2 situation. (Refer to Chapter Six for rules.)

The final drill that we use in teaching the full-court press breaker is called the "full-court press breaker." The squad is divided into two teams—a red team, O, and blue team, X. Each team will play offense for three minutes and defense for three minutes. The defense will set up in a press of my own choosing. The offense will use our full-court press breaker.

The scoring will be as follows: "The offense will get two points per basket. They will get one point for attacking the press, but not having seen any scoring opportunity develop, they set up in our regular offensive set. The whistle will stop play once we get into our regular offensive set. And remember to hustle into your offensive set should we not get a scoring opportunity off the break! Should you make a poor decision and attempt to force a scoring opportunity that has not developed, the defense will get five points—two points for the basket we should have made, two points for the basket they will have the opportunity of mak-

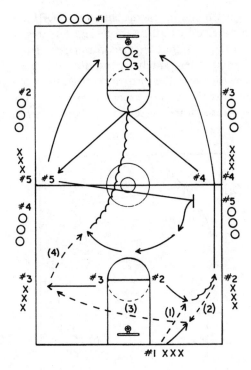

Diagram 11-17. "Three-on-Two Press Breaker"

ing, and one point for the foul shot they may get from having our team in a desperate defensive situation.

"The defense will get further points in these ways: two points per basket; one point for a steal; and two points for a five or ten-second count. However, should the defense try to force a scoring opportunity after a steal instead of setting up in our regular offense, they too will lessen their chance of winning by having five points awarded to the opposing team!"

The coach may rotate players at all positions or he/she may choose to keep players at the positions they will be assigned to in the "ideal" game situation.

The clock will not run continually during this drill, but stop and start as in a game situation. This gives the coach time to discuss miscues in execution, poor selection of the options available, etc. After each team has played on offense for three minutes and defense for three minutes, the losing team will have to run. Remember that in the case of a tie, both teams will have to run.

The same principles that were used in developing our full-court press breaker will be applied to our method of attacking the half-court, and in some instances, the three-quarter court press. There will, however, be minor adjustments in the decisions that will have to be made in regard to what a particular half or three-quarter press is wanting us to do. If the half-court press that we encounter is willing to trap us and commit themselves to their sideline, middle, and back floor coverage assignments before we cross the mid-court line, then our plan of attacking the press remains the same—except that we are now setting up in our initial set positions much closer to our basket (see Diagram 11-18).

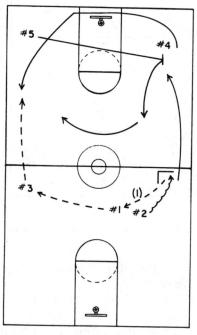

Diagram 11-18. Half-Court Press Breaker with Sideline Option

THE "STACK SERIES" HALF- AND THREE-QUARTER-COURT PRESS BREAKER WITH EIGHT OPTIONS

If the half-court press that we are attacking chooses to force us to cross the mid-court line before setting the trap, we are forced to make some minor adjustments. The first adjustment that we make is in the alignment of our initial set. We stack players #5 and #4 in the middle of the court (see Diagram 11-19). Player #2 positions herself along the sideline near the mid-court line. Player #3 positions herself along the sideline opposite #2 and will come as low as necessary to assure a safe reverse pass out of the trap. Looking over her shoulder toward the stack formation, player #1 initiates the break by dribbling toward the mid-court line staying as close to the outside line of the mid-court circle as possible.

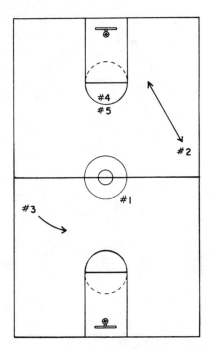

**Diagram 11-19. Initial Stack Set for Half and Three-Quarter
Court Press Breaker**

When she raises her left hand, this signals player #4 to cut to an area along the sideline. It also signals player #2 to start a series of backdoor cuts to the basket and then back out to her original position along the ball-side sideline. Our first option is ball reversal. Player #1 passes the ball to player #3. She, in turn, quickly passes the ball to #4.

Upon receiving the pass, player #4 drives hard toward the basket looking to capitalize on a 2-on-1 situation with player #2, who is sprinting toward the goal down the opposite sideline. This is called "sideline" option (see Diagram 11-20).

Should the defense be determined to stop the pass to player #3, #1 may fire a cross-court pass to player #4 along the sideline. This is called a "sideline bomb" option (see Diagram 11-21). Should the defense choose to deny the reverse action pass to player #3 and cheat with the back defensive player to stop the "sideline bomb" option, player #1 may use a baseball pass to hit player #5 breaking toward the basket down the middle of the floor. This is called a "middle bomb" option (see Diagram 11-22). These two options, referred to as "bomb" options, require longer passes than we prefer to use in breaking the press. We use these options sparingly after all other means of attacking the press have been exhausted.

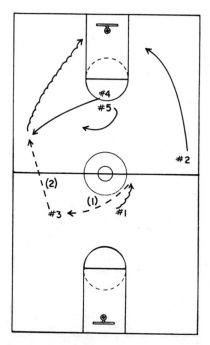

Diagram 11-20. "Sideline" Option out of Stack Series

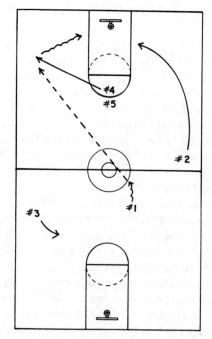

Diagram 11-21. Sideline "Bomb" Option out of Stack Series

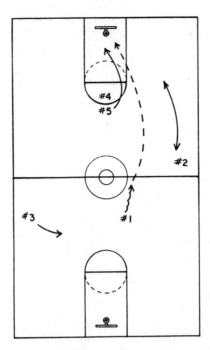

Diagram 11-22. Middle "Bomb" Option out of Stack Series

Our second preferred option is to pass the ball from player #1 or player #3 to player #5 who has been asking for the ball in the middle of the court. Upon receiving the ball, player #5 drives hard down the middle of the court hoping to capitalize on a 3-on-2 situation with player #4 and player #2 who have filled the side lanes. This is called a "middle" option (see Diagram 11-23).

Our third option, called the "dribble" option, occurs when the defense has sagged back on players #4 and #5 to stop the "sideline" and "middle" options. Upon recognizing this sagging defensive tactic, player #3 drives hard toward the middle of the court hoping to capitalize on a 3-on-2 situation with players #4 and #2 who have once again filled the side lanes (see Diagram 11-24).

Our fourth option is referred to as the "strongside" option. This option develops when the strongside defenders are "lulled" into thinking that player #2 is merely serving as a decoy for our plan of attack. Player #2 breaks down the sideline as player #1 approaches the mid-court line. Player #1 fires a pass to player #2 who drives hard toward the basket to set up a 2-on-1 scoring opportunity with player #4. An additional option off this "strongside" attack is called "post." Upon approaching the mid-court line, player #1 notices that #2 is not being denied the pass

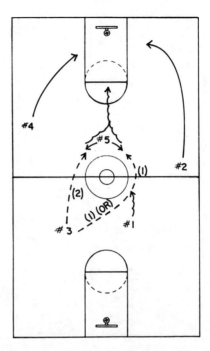

Diagram 11-23. "Middle" Option out of Stack Series

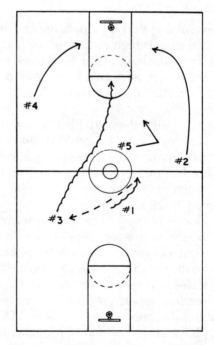

Diagram 11-24. "Dribble" Option out of Stack Series

in the area near the time-line. A quick bounce pass to #2 often brings the defense running, as the ball is now in a very favorable trapping area of the court. Player #5 peels off #4's screen and slides down the side of the key asking for the ball. A quick pass to #5 in the post area results in an easy bucket over the sole back defender or a 2-on-1 situation created by #4 sliding down the key on the opposite side (see Diagrams 11-25 and 11-26).

A fifth option often develops when the defense tries to use man-for-man coverage of the four players in the front court, with the exception of one defensive player who positions herself in the lane to act as a safety. Upon seeing this type of defensive strategy, player #1 drives hard for the basket down the middle of the court hoping to capitalize on a 3-on-2 situation with players #4 and #2. We refer to this as our "penetration" option (see Diagram 11-27).

This same stack series is used against three-quarter court presses that play what we refer to as "soft"—not interested in forcing an interception on the press, but containing with such expertise and patience that frequent 10-second violations occur. The initial set is set up at mid-court or it is adjusted according to where the defense wants to trap.

The same drills used to teach the full-court press breaker are used in teaching the half-court and three-quarter-court press breaker to our

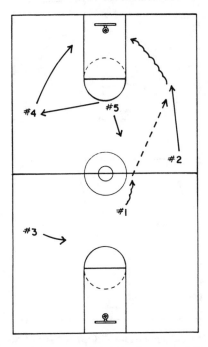

Diagram 11-25. "Strongside" Option out of Stack Series

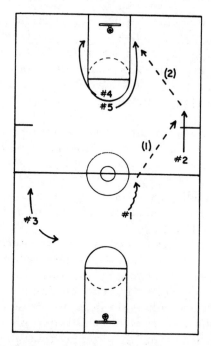

Diagram 11-26. Strongside "Post" Option out of Stack Series

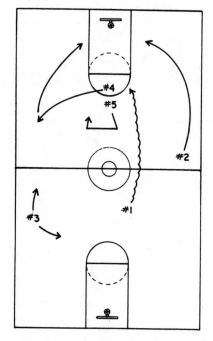

Diagram 11-27. "Penetration" Option out of Stack Series

players. They are, of course, practiced against various types of half-court and three-quarter-court presses.

Frequent repetition of these drills teaches the players our philosophy and techniques used in breaking the press. The competitive design of these drills not only lessens the boredom of repetition, but encourages players to give 100% effort in performing these drills, thus enhancing the effectiveness of our method of breaking the press.

12

Applying the Philosophy of Competition to Scrimmage Situations

Thus far, the motivation of competition has been described only as we use it in our drills. The same principles, however, may be applied to scrimmage situations. To understand fully our methods of scoring during scrimmages, it is necessary to discuss our offensive philosophy and the concepts we employ in building our offensive attack.

SEVEN SHELL DRILLS FOR BUILDING AN OFFENSE

Offensively, we run a variety of sets that follow certain rules of execution. For instance, regardless of the offensive set we are running, whenever the high post player gets the ball, she is to turn and face the basket, and the low post player is to cut. This type of execution must be automatic, so we have devised a series of drills which teach these basic offensive concepts. We refer to them as "shell drills" because they are first taught and practiced without the defense during our Tuesday-Thursday Offensive Workout Sessions. Once execution is mastered, defensive play is added to the drills.

Hi-Lo Action Drill

The first drill is called "Hi-Lo Action" (see Diagram 12-1). Player #1 initiates the drill by taking the ball to the side. Upon reaching the time-line, she begins her approach to an area we call the "magic square"—the ideal feeding area from which we like to initiate our offense (see Diagram 12-2). She uses a "crab dribble approach" if necessary. In this approach—used when under heavy pressure to protect the dribble—the point guard aims her left foot and shoulder toward the magic square and uses a shuffle approach dribbling the ball with her right hand right between her knees. She is staring at the weakside, thus "freezing" the defense—forcing them to maintain coverage of the weakside players, and thereby not allowing them to cheat over to help defend action on the strongside. Over her shoulder, she studies the strongside.

Once the point guard begins to face the weakside, this signals the weakside post player to "flash" to the strongside high post area. The strongside low post player "shapes up" tough looking for the pass from the point guard.

Once the pass goes in to the high post player, she is to pivot so as

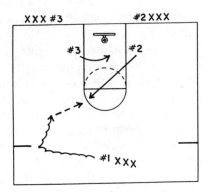

Diagram 12-1. "Hi-Lo Action" Drill

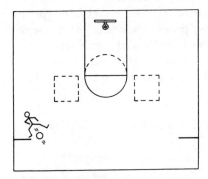

Diagram 12-2. Crab Dribble Approach to "Magic Square"

not to turn her back to the basket. Under heavy pressure, she is to reverse pivot on the foot farthest from the basket. This allows her to step back from her defender and square to the basket. When there is little pressure, the high post player is to forward pivot on the foot closest to the basket. This gives her the ability to either pass or shoot quickly upon squaring to the basket. (Remember that when you forward pivot, it is as if a string was tied to the front of your shirt and was pulling you in the direction you need to go. In the reverse pivot, you should pretend that the string is tied to the back of your shirt to pull you backward.)

As the high post player prepares to square, the low post fakes a "backdoor" cut and then cuts over the top of her defender, sliding across the key looking for the pass from the high post. If the high post cannot pass the ball in to the low post cutting, she may drive to the basket or shoot from the free throw line.

Upon passing the ball in to the high post, the point guard fakes a cut to the basket and then "backpedals" to the mid-court circle to maintain floor balance.

Three minutes are put on the clock. Players will rotate from line #1 to #2 to #3 then back to #1. The scoring is awarded by the coach's subjective critique of each trio's performance on a scale of zero to five . . . 0 points: terrible; 1 point: poor; 2 points: not good; 3 points: average; 4 points: good; 5 points: fantastic! The coach will holler out the points awarded to the scorekeepers as the drill is in progress. At the end of a minute and a half, the drill will be initiated to the other side.

Players are motivated to perform correctly as a score below 3 means that they will have to run a sprint before rotating to the next line. The challenge that they have to meet as a team is set by the coach prior to the drill. For instance, the coach may say that 25 points must be awarded by the end of the three-minute drill or the entire team will have to run six sprints. The greatest motivator, however, is the issuance of game equipment accessories. Upon satisfactory execution of the "Hi-Lo Action" drill, the player will be issued a travel bag. Just as game shorts, shirts, etc., were earned by proper execution of defensive stances, the proper execution of these shell drills will earn players such accessories as travel bags, red shoe laces, leather (instead of canvas) tennis shoes, etc. (Refer to Chapters One and Six for video tape evaluations of practice sessions, execution checklists, etc.)

HI-LO ACTION DRILL CHECKLIST

GUARD POSITION

Code	Improper Execution
GCH	Failure to initiate dribble with correct hand
GHU	Failure to keep head up while dribbling
GPB	Failure to protect the ball while dribbling
GCD	Failure to control defender in approaching the "magic square" (have to be willing to penetrate)
GTB	Turning back to defender on the approach to the "magic square"
GSF	Failure to see the whole floor
GF	Failure to "freeze" the weakside defender(s)
GWH	Dribbling with the wrong hand in approaching the "magic square" (have to "crab" dribble if necessary)
GK	Killing the dribble before you are ready to feed
GPP	Poor passing ability
GBP	Failure to "backpedal" to mid-court circle to stop fast break

HIGH POST POSITION

HSUL	Failure to "shape up" properly at low post
HTF	Failure to time "flash" to high post
HSUH	Failure to shape up properly at high post
HFS	"Flashing" too slowly
HW	Failure to work to get open at high post
HPT	Failure to give a good passing target
HOS	Failure to look over shoulder upon receiving the ball
HRP	Failure to react (adjust) to the pressure
HPOP	Failure to protect the ball on the pivot
HP	Failure to pivot correctly
HS	Failure to square to the basket
HPP	Poor passing ability
HFP	Failure to fake pass
HTT	Failure to assume triple-threat position
HLB	Failure to look at basket (play the rim!)
HFD	Failure to fake defender
HSB	Failure to go "strong" to the basket
HPOS	Failure to protect the ball on the shot
HRP	Failure to get good rebound position
HR	Failure to take the ball back up on a rebound

LOW POST POSITION

LSUL	Failure to "shape up" properly at low post
LFC	Failure to fake on cut
LTC	Failure to time cut
LT	Failure to give target on cut
LPH	Failure to keep defensive player pinned on hip
LPB	Failure to protect the ball
LTA	Failure to turn away from defense on the shot
LS	Failure to square on shot

LGS   Failure to go up strong on the shot

LBF   Putting ball on the floor unnecessarily

LRP   Failure to work to get good rebound position

LR   Failure to take ball back up on rebound

MISTAKE COMMON TO ALL THREE POSITIONS: These will be preceded by G, H, or L TRAVELING

_TS   Traveling by shuffling your feet

_TC   Traveling by changing pivot feet

_TJ   Traveling by picking up pivot foot on jab fake

Pass Opposite Drill

The next drill that we use to teach a basic offensive concept is called "pass opposite." (see Diagram 12-3). This set requires two guards and a weakside low post player. Once again, the point guard initiates the dribble to the side and then approaches the magic square. The approach signals the weakside low post to flash to the high post area. Upon receiving the ball, she squares to the basket following the same pivot foot rules as described in the hi-lo action drill.

The weakside guard moves toward the ball as the dribbler initiates the dribble toward the time-line. As the dribbler makes her approach toward the magic square, she moves away from the ball. On the pass to the high post, she fakes a strongside cut and then cuts sharply to the weakside area along the side of the lane 12 feet to 15 feet away from the basket. As she prepares to receive the pass, she takes a giant step toward the basket with her leg closest to the baseline. She squares to the basket and shoots the jumper. The high post goes to the basket to establish

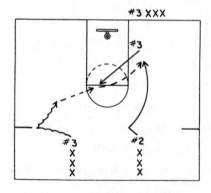

Diagram 12-3. Pass Opposite Drill

good rebound position. The point guard once again fakes a cut to the basket, then backpedals to the mid-court circle to maintain floor balance.

PASS OPPOSITE DRILL CHECKLIST

(The point guard position and high post position are the same as for the Hi-Lo drill)

WEAKSIDE GUARD POSITION

Code	Improper Execution
WFC	Failure to fake cut
WT	Failure to time receiving the ball
WGT	Failure to give target
WTC	Receiving the ball too close to the basket
WGS	Failure to take giant step toward the basket
WSU	Failure to go straight up on shot
WCB	Failure to control body on shot
WFT: WFS	Failure to follow through first; follow shot second
WRP	Failure to work to get rebound position
WR	Failure to take ball back up on rebound

Wing Penetration Drill

Wing Penetration is a drill designed to teach the low post where to go if the wing player should initiate a drive to the key (see Diagram 12-4). The point guard initiates the dribble toward the time-line. The strongside wing player moves toward the baseline as the dribbler

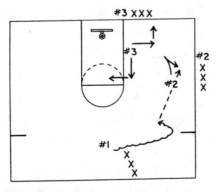

Diagram 12-4. Wing Penetration Drill

approaches her area. As the dribbler starts her approach toward the magic square, the wing player makes a sharp cut toward the sideline to receive the pass from the point guard. As she receives the ball, she squares to the basket using the rules on pivoting as described for the high post in the Hi-Lo Action drill. She jab fakes and drives hard toward the basket.

If the drive is toward the baseline, the low post takes two sliding steps up the lane and one toward the key to position herself for a "dump" pass from the penetrating wing. Upon receiving the pass, she should be square to the basket and put the shot up.

If the drive is toward the middle of the key, the low post takes two sliding steps up the baseline away from the basket and one sliding step toward the baseline looking for the dump. Once again, she should square toward the basket in receiving the pass, so she is ready to shoot.

The sliding action of the low post on wing penetration is called "popping" action—she either pops up and in or out and away depending on the direction of penetration. The point guard once again fakes the cut and "backpedals" to the mid-court circle.

WING PENETRATION DRILL CHECKLIST

LOW POST POSITION

Code	Improper Execution
LSUL	Failure to shape up properly at low post
LF	Failure to fake before popping out or popping up
LTP	Failure to time popping action
LWD	Wrong decision in popping action
LT	Failure to give target on pop out or pop up
LPB	Failure to protect the ball on the pass
LS	Failure to square prior to receiving the pass
LSU	Failure to go straight up on shot
LCB	Failure to control body on shot
LFT: LFS	Failure to follow through first; follow shot second
LRP	Failure to work to get rebound position
LR	Failure to take ball back up on rebound

WING POSITION

WFT	Failure to start off free throw line extended
WF	Failure to "float" as guard approaches
WHM	Failure to work in a horizontal motion to get the pass

(fake the backdoor, spin, scrape off defender on low post, etc.)

WTP	Failure to step toward the pass
WT	Failure to give target
WTR	Failure to time receiving the pass
WPC	Failure to pivot correctly
WS	Failure to square to the basket
WLB	Failure to look at the basket (Play the rim!)
WJB	Failure to give a good jab fake
WP	Failure to penetrate tough
WPB	Failure to protect the ball
WHF	Failure to use head fake before passing
WSBP	Failure to shovel or bounce pass
WRP	Failure to work to get rebound position
WR	Failure to take ball back up on rebound

Low Post Penetration Drill

The "Low Post Penetration" drill is designed to teach the high post where to go once the ball has penetrated into the low post area. This drill is identical to the "Hi-Lo Action" drill, except that this time the drill begins with a wing pass to the low post player who power moves to the basket. The high post steps into the key and spreads out wide at the bottom of the jump-ball circle looking for a "dump" pass from the low post or simply establishing good rebound position (see Diagram 12-5).

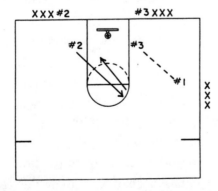

Diagram 12-5. Low Post Penetration Drill

LOW POST PENETRATION DRILL CHECKLIST

LOW POST POSITION

Code	Improper Execution
LSU	Failure to shape up properly
LMF	Failure to move feet to keep defender behind
LA	Failure to stay in low post area
LP	Failure to pin if defender fronts
LTB	Failure to turn back on pin
LHP	Failure to hold pin until ball passes over the defender's head
LT	Failure to give target
LEL	Pushing off with elbow
LOS	Failure to look over shoulder toward middle
LDS	Failure to drop step correctly
LHS	Failure to use head and shoulder fake
LSB	Failure to shovel or bounce pass
LPB	Failure to protect the ball
LGS	Failure to go up strong on shot
LRP	Failure to work to get rebound position
LR	Failure to take ball back up on rebound

HIGH POST POSITION

Code	Improper Execution
HSUL	Failure to shape up properly at low post
HTF	Failure to time flash to high post
HSUH	Failure to shape up properly at high post

(Should the high post get the ball, the rules would become the same as in hi-lo action drill.)

Code	Improper Execution
HBC	Failure to go to bottom of circle
HSO	Failure to spread out at bottom of circle
HGS	Failure to go up strong on shot
HRP	Failure to work to get rebound position
HR	Failure to take the ball back up on the rebound

WING POSITION

WFT	Failure to start off at the free throw line extended
WS	Failure to square to the basket
WTT	Failure to get in triple-threat position
WLB	Failure to look at the basket (play the rim!)
WSD	Failure to shorten the distance between target and defender
WPP	Failure to use three passing points
WT	Telegraphing passes
WF	Failure to float on double team of post

Switch Out Drill

The "switch out" drill is used to teach the players how to pop out a post to the wing position. The first part of the drill is identical to the "wing penetration" drill, but instead of penetrating the low post area, the wing, after having looked inside, will pass the ball back to the point guard and go screen for the low post. The low post fakes opposite to keep her defender busy as the screen is being set, and then scrapes her defender off on the screen set by the wing player and pops out to the wing position. She now assumes the responsibilities of the wing player as described in the "wing penetration" drill. As the post goes by the wing screen, the wing will open up toward the ball looking for a quick pass should the defense have miscued, then assumes the responsibilities of the strongside low post as described in the "wing penetration" drill (see Diagram 12-6).

The point guard follows the same rules as described in the Hi-Lo Action drill, until she has passed the ball to the wing. She must then work to get herself open for the return pass from the wing. She must

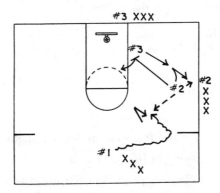

Diagram 12-6. Switch Out Drill

square to the basket pretending to read the defense before passing it to the low post popping out to the wing position. She then backpedals to the mid-court circle to maintain floor balance.

SWITCH-OUT DRILL CHECKLIST

GUARD POSITION

(The first part of the drill will have the guard following the same rules as in Hi-Lo Action.)

Code	Improper Execution
GPR	Failure to prepare to receive the pass back (fake down or weakside, spin, etc.)
GS	Failure to square upon receiving the return pass
GTT	Failure to get in triple-threat position if necessary
GLB	Failure to look at basket (play the rim!)
GPP	Poor passing ability
GFP	Forcing the pass
GBP	Failure to backpedal to mid-court circle to stop fast break

WING POSITION

(The first part of the drill will have the wing following the same rules as in "wing penetration.")

WPP	Poor passing ability
WF	Failure to fake before screening
WSP	Failure to screen properly
WOU	Failure to open up toward ball properly
WSU	Failure to shape up on low post

(Once the wing has established herself as the low post, the same rules would be followed as described in the wing penetration drill/post penetration drill.)

LOW POST POSITION

LSU	Failure to shape up properly
LMF	Failure to move feet to keep defender behind
LA	Failure to stay in low post area
LFO	Failure to fake opposite to occupy defender before the screen is set
LSD	Failure to scrape off defender on screen

(Once the post has established herself as the wing player, the same rules would be followed as described in the wing penetration drill.)

Guard Cut, Fill, and Turn Drill

The "Guard Cut, Fill, and Turn" drill teaches players how to stay equidistant apart on the perimeter, how to cut, how to fill, and how to turn the floor (see Diagram 12-7). The guard initiates play by dribbling toward one of the wing players. The strongside wing player floats toward the baseline looking for a pass. The weakside guard moves in the same direction as the dribbler ready to fill the spot vacated by the point guard. Upon passing the ball to the strongside wing, the point guard cuts to the basket looking for a return pass. The weakside wing fills the point guard spot. After looking inside at the cutter, player #2 passes the ball out to player #3 and then moves along the baseline to the other side of the court. Not having received the ball on the cut, player #1 cuts through the lane filling #3's vacated area. She receives the pass from #3 and then fires the ball to #2, the baseline player, who takes the shot. Player #3 crashes the weakside board and player #1 backpedals to the mid-court circle to maintain floor balance.

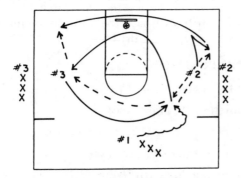

Diagram 12-7. Guard Out, Fill and Turn Drill

GUARD CUT, FILL, AND TURN DRILL CHECKLIST

GUARD POSITION

(The first part of the drill will have the guard following the same rules as described in the Hi-Lo Action drill.)

Code	Improper Execution
GPC	Failure to fake opposite before cut
GTC	Failure to time cut
GT	Failure to give target on cut

GCS	Failure to cut sharply and with purpose
GCL	Failure to clear lane quickly
GPR	Failure to prepare to receive the pass back
GS	Failure to square on return pass
GTT	Failure to get in triple-threat position
GLB	Failure to look at basket (play the rim!)
GPP	Poor passing ability
GFP	Forcing the pass
GBP	Failure to backpedal to mid-court circle to stop the fast break

STRONGSIDE WING POSITION

(The first part of the drill will have the wing following the same rules as in wing penetration.)

SWTS	Flashing along baseline too slowly
SWT	Failure to give target
SWGS	Failure to take "giant step" toward basket on return pass

(The last part of the drill will have the wing following the same rules as described in the Pass Opposite drill.)

WEAKSIDE WING POSITION

WWF	Failure to fake before filling
WWFS	Failure to fill cutter's spot
WWPR	Failure to prepare to receive return pass
WWS	Failure to square to the basket
WWTT	Failure to assume triple-threat position if necessary
WWLB	Failure to look at the basket (play the rim!)
WWPP	Poor passing ability
WWFP	Forcing the pass
WWRP	Failure to fight for rebound position
WWR	Failure to put ball back up on rebound

Triple Post Rotation Drill

The final shell drill that we employ to teach the cutting action of our overload or triple post set is called the "Triple Post Rotation" drill. If the coach passes the ball in to the low post, she uses a power move to

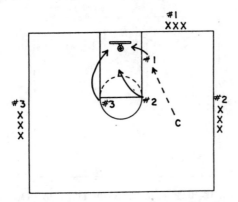

Diagram 12-8. Pass to Low Post Option

take it to the basket; the strongside high post goes to the bottom of the jump-ball circle; and the weakside high post goes to the weakside rebound position (see Diagram 12-8). If the coach passes the ball in to the strongside high post, she turns to face the basket. The low post cuts across the lane; the weakside high post cuts diagonally after the low post cuts; and the low post "loops" back around the diagonal cutter using her as a screen to get the ball in the middle of the key (see Diagram 12-9). If the coach passes the ball in to the weakside high post, the same rules are followed. The high post turns to face the basket; the low post cuts across; the strongside post cuts diagonally; and the low post loops back around the diagonal cutter to receive the pass (see Diagram 12-10).

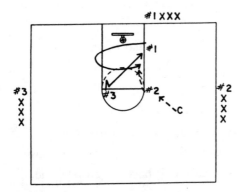

Diagram 12-9. Pass to Strongside High Post Option

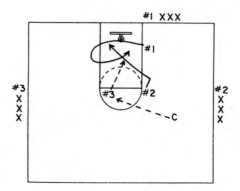

Diagram 12-10. Pass to Weakside High Post Option

TRIPLE POST ROTATION DRILL CHECKLIST

"Pass to Low Post Option"

(Low Post Position—Follows the same rules as in "Low Post Penetration" drill.)

(Strongside High Post—Follows the same rules as in last part of "Low Post Penetration" drill.)

WEAKSIDE HIGH POST POSITION

Code	Improper Execution
WHSU	Failure to shape up properly
WHRP	Failure to work to get rebound position
WHR	Failure to take the ball back up on the rebound

"Pass to Strong Side High Post Option"

(Low Post Position—Follows same rules as low post in "Hi-Lo Action" drill in the first part of this drill.)

LL	Failure to loop diagonal cutter properly
LPB	Failure to protect the ball
LTA	Failure to turn away from the defense on the shot
LS	Failure to square on the shot
LGS	Failure to go up strong on the shot
LRP	Failure to work to get good rebound position
LR	Failure to take ball back up on rebound

(Strongside High Post Position—Follows the same rules as in "Hi-Lo Action" drill.)

WEAKSIDE HIGH POST POSITION

WHSU	Failure to shape up properly
WHB	Failure to fake backdoor cut
WHD	Failure to time diagonal cut after low post cut
WHT	Failure to give target on cut
WHCS	Failure to cut sharply and with purpose
WHS	Failure to square on the shot
WHGS	Failure to go up strong on the shot
WHRP	Failure to work to get good rebound position
WHR	Failure to take ball back up on rebound

"Pass to Weakside High Post Option"

(Low Post Position—Follows same rules as for "Pass to Strongside High Post Option.")

(Strongside High Post Position—Follows the same rules as weakside high post in "Pass to Strongside High Post Option.")

(Weakside High Post Position—Follows same rules as in "Hi-Lo Action" Drill.)

All of our shell drills are three-minute drills with all players rotating to all positions. After one and a half minutes, they are run to the other side, so that execution may be practiced from both sides. The scoring and running stipulations for all drills are the same as that described in the "Hi-Lo Action" drill.

HALF-COURT SCRIMMAGE WORK

Once these basic offensive concepts have been mastered, they must be implemented into the execution of our five-on-five offensive sets. We like to practice our offensive patterns in half-court scrimmage situations with the blue team, X, on offense for two and a half minutes, and the red team, O, on defense. The last two and a half minutes, the teams change from offense to defense.

The most critical factors of a half-court scrimmage is that it must be as similar to a game situation as possible, or bad habits will be formed. We always have the offense start the scrimmage out of bounds on the sideline. We are insistent that we always look to score off of our sideline play (see Diagrams 12-11 and 12-12). If no scoring opportunity is available, the playmaker hollers "Set up!" and the offensive players go to their assigned positions to start the play. If execution of the sideline play was acceptable even though they did not score off of it, but at least

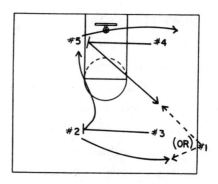

Diagram 12-11. "Sideline" Play

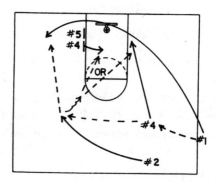

Diagram 12-12. "Sideline" Play (Continued)

looked at it, the coach awards the team one point by hollering "Point!"

The scorekeepers put one point up for the offensive team. Had they scored on the play, two points would have been awarded if the coach felt that execution was acceptable and not forced. Should execution be unacceptable, but a basket made in spite of sloppy execution and poor decision making, it is counted as only one point and is so signaled to the scorekeepers by the coach hollering "Luck!"

All points are awarded to the offensive team in this manner—one point for acceptable execution even if a basket isn't scored signaled by "Point!"; two points per basket made if execution is acceptable; and one point per made basket if execution is unacceptable signaled by "Luck!" Let us say that while running the pattern the high post gets the ball and the low post cuts before the high post squares to the basket, thus ruining any hi-lo action. The high post player scores on a jumper off the free throw line. The coach hollers "Luck!" and quickly explains, "Don't cut until the high post turns to see you."

Defensively, points are awarded in a similar fashion. One point is awarded for every defensive rebound and steal, provided that the other four players break out to the four spots which need to be filled to initiate the fast break successfully (refer to Chapter Nine), and that the ball is brought up to the mid-court line in our prescribed fashion of initiating the fast break. If execution is acceptable, the coach will holler "One!"; if it is unacceptable, the coach will holler "None!"

After each team has played offense and defense for two and a half minutes, the losing team has to run a horse. Five more minutes are put on the clock and another offensive pattern is practiced; and once again, play begins with the ball being thrown in from the sideline and the possibility of scoring off of it is checked out before setting up in the offensive set.

This is not to say that we do all of our half-court work in this manner. Once the team gains experience in executing our basic offensive concepts and shows the maturity to be willing to execute them according to the plans of their coach—not what is easy or seems best to them—we change our method of scoring. We award one point per basket, two points if fouled on the shot, and no defensive points. The losing team must run at the end of the five-minute period.

Sometimes we allow the defense to score only if they can success-fully fast break to the other end of the court. In other words, the offensive team is working on a particular offensive pattern on the half-court. When the defensive team gains possession of the ball on a steal or defensive rebound, they are to try to score using the fast break down on the other end of the court. They are awarded one point per basket if they score on the break; they are also awarded one point if upon seeing that their fast break efforts have been thwarted, they holler "Set up!" and go to their positions of the offensive set. This keeps a team from forcing the fast break.

Because of our aggressive style of play, my teams have had more trouble with forcing the break than they have with reluctance to carry it out when the opportunity was there. A coach must adjust his/her method of motivational scoring to suit the needs of his/her personnel.

Another problem that can often arise is "one-sidedness"—if you like to have your best five practice as a unit against your second or third team. I prefer this method as it allows players to learn to work together as a unit. If my depth is good, I also like to employ a platoon method with the second team playing six minutes of the second quarter of every game. This certainly promotes team morale and puts the burden of responsibility upon ten players instead of five. Oftentimes, however, a weaker unit will not put forth a good effort in a half-court or full-court scrimmage session because they figure they will lose and have to run anyway. To offset the stronger team's advantage, the coach will award the weaker unit 8, 10, etc., points before play begins. This often encourages the second team to work harder in protecting their lead, and it always pushes the strongest five to do their best in overcoming the deficit imposed upon them.

FULL-COURT SCRIMMAGE WORK

Many of the same methods used in our half-court scrimmage sessions will, of course, be used in our full-court work. There are special methods, however, that may be employed to improve the full-court effort.

Five minutes are put on the clock. Both teams are instructed as to the offensive pattern and defensive strategy they are to use. For instance, the blue team may be told that they are to run a full-court 1-2-2 trapping press allowing the first pass to come in. Once the ball penetrates below the free throw line, they are to set up in a 1-3-1 zone which will trap in the corners. The red team may be instructed to run pressure man-for-man defense full court. Offensively, the blue team is to run our "Guard Cut" offensive pattern and the red team is to run our "1-4" offense.

First of all, the team gaining possession of the ball on the center jump must try to score off of our jump-ball play (see Diagram 12-13). Just as in the half-court scrimmage, a scoring opportunity may not develop, but they must look at it before setting up in their offensive pattern.

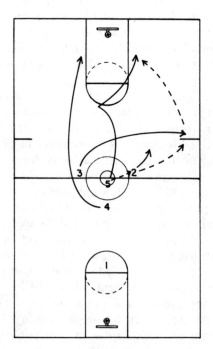

Diagram 12-13. "Jump Ball" Play . . . . Center Court

Since both teams are to use a lot of pressure in playing defense, the coach may award five-second held ball violations and ten-second back-court violations with points on the scoreboard. We award three points for a five-second violation and five points for a ten-second backcourt violation.

We are also interested in OER, offensive efficiency rating. Due to the fact that we are so defensive-oriented and award points for defensive performances, we often become unaware of how little offensive output is actually being produced. To create more interest in this area, we position a large blackboard on the side of the court. Each time a team has possession of the ball, a large circle is drawn on the blackboard under the appropriate column of red or blue team. If the team scores on that particular possession, an X is put inside the circle; if the team fails to score, it is left empty. Three empty circles in a row indicates to us that we have failed to score on the last three possessions. The scrimmage is stopped immediately and the guilty team has to run a horse. Other times, we deduct five points off of their score.

Another rule we enforce during our full-court scrimmage session might be that the ball is not allowed to be dribbled across the mid-court line in an area known as "no-man's land" (see Diagram 12–14). It is an area which extends from time-line to time-line and six feet out from the

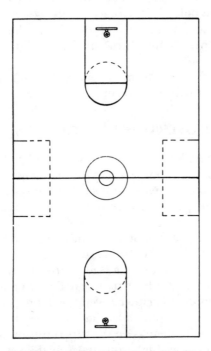

Diagram 12-14. "No-Man's Land"

sideline toward the middle of the court. We feel that this is a prime trapping area. So in order to avoid this costly mistake, we make the entire team run if the rule is violated or we deduct five points from their score.

THE DELAY GAME PRACTICE SESSION

We use two types of delay tactics in our game situations: one to run time off the clock; the other to bring a team out of its zone forcing them to pick us up man-for-man. Each of these situations, therefore, must be practiced in a different way.

When we are trying to run time off the clock, we set up our scrimmage in the following fashion: Two minutes are put up on the clock. The red team will be on offense only. Points will be awarded in this manner—3 points for every 10 consecutive seconds run off the clock; 2 points for every made basket; and 3 points for every made free throw.

Each team has the ball on offense for two minutes with the losing team having to run.

When we are using the delay game to bring a team out of zone coverage, the scrimmage is set up in the following way: Three minutes are put up on the clock. The offensive team spreads out in our delay game offensive set and holds the ball until the defense is forced to come out of its zone as signaled by the coach. Since we are not worried about running out the clock, points are not awarded for holding the ball, but two points for every made free throw, and two points for every offensive rebound.

Once again, after each team has the ball on offense for three minutes, the losing team will have to run.

THE OVERTIME PRACTICE SESSION

Good decision making is the key to successful performances in overtime situations. To predict every situation that may arise in an overtime is virtually impossible; therefore, it is best to put only three minutes on the clock and award points just as they would be awarded in a game situation.

Our strategy will vary in an overtime game due to many factors. If we feel that we are lucky to be in this situation, we will probably try to sit on the ball with or without the lead. With the lead, we go into our delay game. Without the lead, we try to run a very patient offense—such as the weave described in Chapter Seven—as long as we are in striking distance, e.g., one or two points behind. The less time there is on the clock, the more pressure there is on the superior team. It does not matter how fast you run or how high you jump in the waning seconds of a close ball game. The crowd, the referees, team preparation, coaching strategies, and just good old-fashioned luck become factors in the outcome of the game.

If we feel that we are equal to or superior to the team we are playing, we will try to gain the lead and then go into our delay game. Up to the last 45 seconds, every one on the team is allowed to take an unguarded layup. The team "super star" will be allowed to take 7 to 8-foot jump shots and unguarded layups. Once it gets down to 45 seconds, no one is allowed to shoot anything but unguarded layups.

So, the strategy of the game unfolds as it happens, but the decision making of the players should be charted. This is where the chalkboard positioned alongside the court comes into play once again. A subjective scoring of each team's performance will be tallied on the blackboard in much the same fashion as that described in the shell drills. The scale will, however, be in reverse—5 points will be tallied when the coach hollers out "Terrible"; 4 points will be recorded when the decision is "Poor"; 3 points will be marked when the decision is declared, "Not good!"

At the end of the overtime period, the team with the highest score on the blackboard for poor decision making has to run a horse.

These are just a few examples of how you can motivate proper execution, sound decision making, team play, and 100% effort into your practice sessions whether they be in the form of drill or scrimmage work. Competition nurtures a desire to be a winner, not only in sports, but in life itself. The responsible coach will teach his/her players how to compete to the best of their abilities. As a daily reminder of this responsibility, I keep this quote posted on the wall of my office:

"To conquer a nation, you need only to destroy its will to compete!"

Nikita Kruschev, Soviet Leader